はしがき

　本書は第一学習社発行の英語教科書「Vivid English Communication I」に完全準拠したノートです。各パート見開き 2 ページで，主に教科書本文の予習や授業傍用での使用に役立つよう工夫しました。

JN102725

CONTENTS

本書の構成と利用法

本書は教科書本文を完全に理解するための学習の導きをしています。本書を最大限に活用して，教科書本文の理解を深めましょう。

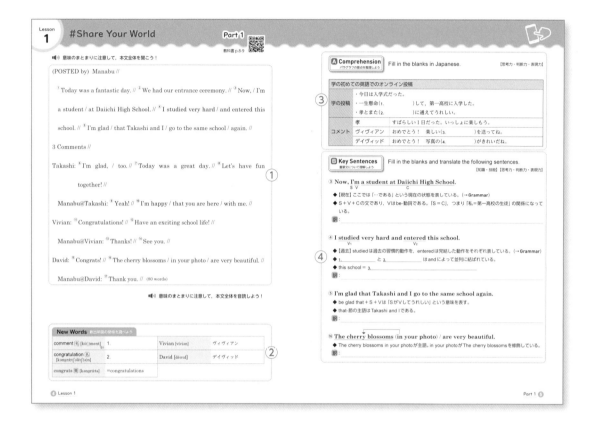

① 教科書本文

意味のまとまりごとにスラッシュ（/）を入れました。ここで示した意味のまとまりを意識しながら音読しましょう。また，学習がしやすいよう，一文ずつ番号を付けました。上部の二次元コードは，本文音声のリスニングや音読に使用できる「スピーキング・トレーナー」にリンクしています。右ページに詳しい解説があります。

※本文中のグレーの網かけは，教科書では印字されておらず，音声としてのみ配信している部分であることを示します。

② New Words

新出単語の意味を調べて，日本語で記入しましょう。単語の品詞と発音記号も示しました。A1〜B2は，CEFR-Jでのレベルを表します。A1（易）〜B2（難）です。

『CEFR-J Wordlist Version 1.6』東京外国語大学投野由紀夫研究室．（URL: http://cefr-j.org/download.htmlより2021年2月ダウンロード）

③ **A** Comprehension

本文のまとめとなる図表を日本語で完成させることで本文の理解を深める問題です。パートごとにさまざまな形の図表を完成させます。

④ **B** Key Sentences

教科書の本文で，新出の文法事項に関連したものや，文構造が複雑なものや指示語を含むものなどを重要文と位置づけ，解説を加えました。解説を日本語や英語で完成させ，和訳をする問題です。日本語を補う問題の解答欄はカッコで，英語を補う問題の解答欄は下線で示しています。

スピーキング・トレーナー

本文の音声データ無料配信，音読用のボイスレコーダーが使用できます。
ブラウザ版とアプリ版 (iOS，Android) をご用意しています。
https://www.daiichi-g.co.jp/sptrainer/

本書の発行終了とともに当サイトを閉鎖することがあります。

アクセスキー　　chk37

音声データ配信

音声をPCやスマートフォンなどから聞くことができます。（PCはブラウザ版のみ対応しています）

＊音声のダウンロードは，PCの場合はブラウザ版，スマートフォンの場合はアプリ版でご利用いただけます。アプリ版ではアプリ内でのみ再生が可能です。

＊アップしてある音声データは著作権法で保護されています。音声データの利用は個人が私的に利用する場合に限られます。データを第三者に提供・販売することはできません。

ボイスレコーダー

音読の学習効果をさらに高めるために，自分の発話の録音ができるボイスレコーダーを用意しました。PCやスマートフォンからご利用できます。

ボイスレコーダーの使用にはユーザーIDとパスワードが必要です。IDとパスワードを自分で設定（半角英数字5文字以上）して，利用を開始してください。

メモ欄

ID	
パスワード	

＊IDとパスワードは紛失しないようにしてください。万が一紛失した場合は，それまでに記録された学習履歴がすべて参照できなくなります。復元はできませんので，ご注意ください。

＊音声データは各レッスンのページに個別に用意した二次元コードを読み取れば，ログインなしで聞くことができます。

＊正常に動作しない場合は「ヘルプ」→「動作要件」をご確認ください。

■情報料は無料ですが，通信費は利用者の負担となります。
■Wi-Fi環境でのご利用を推奨します。
■アプリ版では，教材データのダウンロード時と録音データのアップロード時等に通信が発生します。

🔊 意味のまとまりに注意して，本文全体を聞こう！

(POSTED by) Manabu //

①Today was a fantastic day. // ②We had our entrance ceremony. // ③Now, / I'm

a student / at Daiichi High School. // ④I studied very hard / and entered this

school. // ⑤I'm glad / that Takashi and I / go to the same school / again. //

3 Comments //

Takashi: ⑥I'm glad, / too. // ⑦Today was a great day. // ⑧Let's have fun

together! //

Manabu@Takashi: ⑨Yeah! // ⑩I'm happy / that you are here / with me. //

Vivian: ⑪Congratulations! // ⑫Have an exciting school life! //

Manabu@Vivian: ⑬Thanks! // ⑭See you. //

David: ⑮Congrats! // ⑯The cherry blossoms / in your photo / are very beautiful. //

Manabu@David: ⑰Thank you. // (80 words)

🔊 意味のまとまりに注意して，本文全体を音読しよう！

New Words 新出単語の意味を調べよう			
comment 名 [kɑ́(:)ment] B1	1.	Vivian [víviən]	ヴィヴィアン
congratulation 名 [kəngræt͡ʃəléɪʃ(ə)n]	2.	David [déɪvɪd]	デイヴィッド
congrats 間 [kəngrǽts]	=congratulations		

A Comprehension
パラグラフの要点を整理しよう

Fill in the blanks in Japanese.　　　　　【思考力・判断力・表現力】

学の初めての英語でのオンライン投稿		
学の投稿	・今日は入学式だった。 ・一生懸命(1.　　　　　　)して，第一高校に入学した。 ・孝とまた(2.　　　　　　)に通えてうれしい。	
コメント	孝	すばらしい1日だった。いっしょに楽しもう。
	ヴィヴィアン	おめでとう！　楽しい(3.　　　　　)を送ってね。
	デイヴィッド	おめでとう！　写真の(4.　　　　　)がきれいだね。

B Key Sentences
重要文について理解しよう

Fill in the blanks and translate the following sentences.
【知識・技能】【思考力・判断力・表現力】

③ Now, I'm a student at Daiichi High School.
　　　　S　V　　　　　　C

◆【現在】ここでは「…である」という現在の状態を表している。（→ Grammar）

◆ S＋V＋Cの文であり，Vはbe-動詞である。「S＝C」，つまり「私＝第一高校の生徒」の関係になっている。

訳：＿＿＿＿＿＿＿＿＿＿＿＿＿＿＿＿＿＿＿＿＿＿＿＿＿＿＿＿

④ I studied very hard and entered this school.
　　　V1　　　　　　　　　V2

◆【過去】studiedは過去の習慣的動作を，enteredは完結した動作をそれぞれ表している。（→ Grammar）

◆ 1.＿＿＿＿＿＿＿　と 2.＿＿＿＿＿＿＿　はandによって並列に結ばれている。

◆ this school ＝ 3.＿＿＿＿＿＿＿＿＿＿＿＿＿

訳：＿＿＿＿＿＿＿＿＿＿＿＿＿＿＿＿＿＿＿＿＿＿＿＿＿＿＿＿

⑤ I'm glad that Takashi and I go to the same school again.

◆ be glad that＋S＋Vは「SがVしてうれしい」という意味を表す。

◆ that-節の主語はTakashi and Iである。

訳：＿＿＿＿＿＿＿＿＿＿＿＿＿＿＿＿＿＿＿＿＿＿＿＿＿＿＿＿

⑯ The cherry blossoms (in your photo) / are very beautiful.

◆ The cherry blossoms in your photoが主語。in your photoがThe cherry blossomsを修飾している。

訳：＿＿＿＿＿＿＿＿＿＿＿＿＿＿＿＿＿＿＿＿＿＿＿＿＿＿＿＿

教科書 p.10-11

🔊 意味のまとまりに注意して，本文全体を聞こう！

1 ①Social media are an important part / of our daily lives / today. // ②In fact, / these useful tools / make our lives very exciting. // ③However, / keep some rules in mind / when you use social media. //

2 ④First, / pay attention / to personal privacy. // ⑤Don't post private information / about you and your friends. // ⑥If a bad person finds the information, / you and your friends / will have some problems. //

3 ⑦Second, / don't use social media / for many hours / every day. // ⑧You will easily become a social media addict. // ⑨Sometimes / put down your smartphone / and look at the real world / with your own eyes. // (95 words)

🔊 意味のまとまりに注意して，本文全体を音読しよう！

New Words 新出単語の意味を調べよう			
media 名 [míːdiə] B2	1.	privacy 名 [práɪvəsi] B1	2.
private 形 [práɪvət] A2	3.	addict 名 [ǽdɪkt] B2	4.

A Comprehension
パラグラフの要点を整理しよう Fill in the blanks in Japanese.　　　　　　【思考力・判断力・表現力】

SNS…私たちの生活をとても楽しいものにしてくれる便利なツール。 使用にあたっていくつかの(1.　　　　　　　)を覚えておく必要がある。		
ルール① 個人のプライバシーに注意	・自分や友達の(2.　　　　　　)を投稿してはいけない。 → 悪い人に見つかるとトラブルに巻き込まれる。	
ルール② 毎日何時間も使わないこと	・SNS(3.　　　　　　)になってしまう。 → スマートフォンを置いて，(4.　　　　　　)に目を向けよう。	

B Key Sentences
重要文について理解しよう Fill in the blanks and translate the following sentences.
【知識・技能】【思考力・判断力・表現力】

② In fact, these useful tools make our lives very exciting.
　　　　　　　　　　S　　　　　　　V　　　O　　　　C
　◆ S＋V＋O＋Cの文。「O＝C」，つまり「our lives ＝ very exciting」の関係になっている。
　◆ these useful toolsは 1.＿＿＿＿＿＿＿＿＿＿＿＿＿＿ を指す。
　◆ make＋O＋Cで「OをCにする」という意味になる。
　訳：＿＿＿＿＿＿＿＿＿＿＿＿＿＿＿＿＿＿＿＿＿＿＿＿＿＿＿＿＿＿＿

⑤ Don't post private information (about you and your friends).
　◆ Don't ～は否定の命令文であり，「(2.　　　　　　　　　　　)」という意味。
　◆ aboutで始まる前置詞句がprivate informationを修飾している。
　訳：＿＿＿＿＿＿＿＿＿＿＿＿＿＿＿＿＿＿＿＿＿＿＿＿＿＿＿＿＿＿＿

⑥ If a bad person finds the information, / you and your friends will have
　　　　　　　　　　　　　　　　　　　　　　　　　S　　　　　　　　　　V
　　some problems.
　　　　　　O
　◆ if … は条件を表す副詞節であり，「もし…なら」という意味。
　◆ 副詞節は主節を修飾する。この文ではコンマ以降の部分が主節であり，S＋V＋Oになっている。
　◆【未来】will＋動詞の原形で「～でしょう」という未来のことがらを表す。(→ Grammar)
　訳：＿＿＿＿＿＿＿＿＿＿＿＿＿＿＿＿＿＿＿＿＿＿＿＿＿＿＿＿＿＿＿

⑧ You will easily become a social media addict.
　◆【未来】will＋動詞の原形で「～でしょう」という未来のことがらを表す。(→ Grammar)
　　この文ではwillと動詞の原形の間に副詞easilyが挿入されている。
　訳：＿＿＿＿＿＿＿＿＿＿＿＿＿＿＿＿＿＿＿＿＿＿＿＿＿＿＿＿＿＿＿

■)) 意味のまとまりに注意して，本文全体を聞こう！

1 ①How do you use social media? // ②You can share recent events / in your everyday life / with your friends. // ③You can also introduce your favorite shops / and interesting Internet news. //

2 ④On social media, / you can talk / about some social problems, / too. // ⑤Sometimes / you may have an exciting discussion / about such problems / with your friends. //

3 ⑥If you use social media carefully, / they can be a wonderful tool. // ⑦You can communicate / with people / all over the world. // ⑧Now, / why don't you open up a huge new world / in the palm / of your hand? // (90 words)

■)) 意味のまとまりに注意して，本文全体を音読しよう！

New Words 新出単語の意味を調べよう			
recent 形 [ríːs(ə)nt] A2	1.	discussion 名 [dɪskʌʃ(ə)n] A2	2.
palm 名 [páːm] B1	3.		

A Comprehension
パラグラフの要点を整理しよう

Fill in the blanks in Japanese. 【思考力・判断力・表現力】

SNSの使い方	
具体例	・日常生活の最近の(1.　　　　　　　)を友達と共有できる。 ・お気に入りの(2.　　　　　　　)やおもしろいインターネットニュースを紹介できる。 ・(3.　　　　　　　)について話したり，友達と議論ができる。
注意して使えば，すばらしいツールになる。	
具体例	・(4.　　　　　　　)の人々とコミュニケーションをとることができる。

B Key Sentences
重要文について理解しよう

Fill in the blanks and translate the following sentences.
【知識・技能】【思考力・判断力・表現力】

② **You can share recent events (in your everyday life) with your friends.**

◆ share A with B で「AをBと共有する」という意味。

◆ everyday の品詞は(1.　　　　　　　)。副詞句として2語で用いる every day との区別に注意。

訳：＿＿＿＿＿＿＿＿＿＿＿＿＿＿＿＿＿＿＿＿＿＿＿＿＿＿＿＿＿＿＿

⑤ **Sometimes you may have an exciting discussion about such problems with your friends.**

◆【助動詞】助動詞 may は「～かもしれない」という推量を表す。(→ Grammar)

◆ have a discussion about A with B で「AについてBと議論をする」という意味。

◆ such problems ＝ 2.＿＿＿＿＿＿＿＿＿＿＿＿＿＿＿＿＿

訳：＿＿＿＿＿＿＿＿＿＿＿＿＿＿＿＿＿＿＿＿＿＿＿＿＿＿＿＿＿＿＿

⑦ **You can communicate with people all over the world.**

◆【助動詞】助動詞 can は「～できる」という可能を表す。(→ Grammar)

◆ communicate は自動詞であり，communicate with ... で「…とコミュニケーションをとる」の意味。

訳：＿＿＿＿＿＿＿＿＿＿＿＿＿＿＿＿＿＿＿＿＿＿＿＿＿＿＿＿＿＿＿

⑧ **Now, why don't you open up a huge new world in the palm of your hand?**

◆ Why don't you ～? は「～しませんか。」「～してはどうですか。」という提案や勧誘を表す。

◆ in the palm of one's hand は「…の手の(ひらの)中で」という意味。

訳：＿＿＿＿＿＿＿＿＿＿＿＿＿＿＿＿＿＿＿＿＿＿＿＿＿＿＿＿＿＿＿

🔊 意味のまとまりに注意して，本文全体を聞こう！

Vivian: ①Hello, / Kumi! //

Kumi: ②Hi, / Vivian! // ③Welcome / to my house. // ④Come in! //

Vivian: ⑤Thank you. // ⑥What were you doing, / Kumi? //

Kumi: ⑦I was drinking chocolate. //

Vivian: ⑧Oh, / I like hot chocolate! // ⑨It really tastes good! //

Kumi: ⑩Um … / do you know / about the long history / of chocolate? //

Vivian: ⑪I don't know much / about it. // ⑫Please tell me. //

Kumi: ⑬Actually, / people drank chocolate / from very ancient times. // ⑭People

first ate chocolate bars / around 1850. //

Vivian: ⑮Is that right? //

Kumi: ⑯Yeah. // ⑰Manabu and I / are working / on a project / about the history /

of chocolate / for an English class. //

Vivian: ⑱Are you going to give a presentation / in class? //

Kumi: ⑲Yes. // ⑳So / we have to make some good slides. // (103 words)

🔊 意味のまとまりに注意して，本文全体を音読しよう！

New Words 新出単語の意味を調べよう			
um 間 [ʌm]	えーと，うーん	presentation 名 [prèz(ə)ntéɪʃ(ə)n] B1	1.
slide 名 [sláɪd] A2	2.		

 **Comprehension** Fill in the blanks in Japanese. 【思考力・判断力・表現力】

パラグラフの要点を整理しよう

ヴィヴィアンと久美の会話

・ヴィヴィアンが久美の家に着いたとき，久美は (1.　　　　　　) を飲んでいた。

・久美はヴィヴィアンにチョコレートには長い歴史があることを教える。

　┌・古代から人々はチョコレートを (2.　　　　　) いた。

　└・チョコレートバーを食べ始めたのは (3.　　　　　) 頃からである。

・学と久美は，英語の授業でチョコレートの (4.　　　　　) についてのプレゼンテーションをする。

　そのためにスライドを作らなければならない。

B Key Sentences Fill in the blanks and translate the following sentences.

重要文について理解しよう 【知識・技能】【思考力・判断力・表現力】

⑥ **What were you doing, Kumi?**

◆【進行形】過去進行形was [were] ＋〜ingで「(過去のある時点で)〜していた」を表す。(→ **Grammar**)

訳：_____

⑪ **I don't know much about it.**

◆ not ... muchは「あまり…ない」という意味である。

◆ it ＝ 1._____

訳：_____

⑰ **Manabu and I are working on a project (about the history of chocolate)**
　　　S　　　　　　V

for an English class.

◆【進行形】現在進行形am [are, is] ＋〜ingで「(今)〜している」を表す。(→ **Grammar**)

◆ about the history of chocolateが後ろからa projectを修飾している。

訳：_____

_____

⑱ **Are you going to give a presentation in class?**

◆ be going to 〜は「(2.　　　　　　　　　)」という意味で，前から予定している未来の
　ことがらを表す。

訳：_____

I Was Drinking Chocolate!

Part 2

教科書 p.24-25

🔊 意味のまとまりに注意して，本文全体を聞こう！

Kumi: ① Today, / we want / to talk / about the history / of chocolate. // ② Over 3,000 years ago, / people / in Central America / first had wild cacao beans. // ③ People there / started / to grow cacao trees. //

Manabu: ④ From about 250 / to 900 AD, / the Maya used wild cacao beans / as money. // ⑤ They used them / in events / for the gods, / too. // ⑥ Cacao beans were very precious. //

Kumi: ⑦ From about 1200 / to 1500, / the Aztecs used cacao beans / to pay taxes. // ⑧ In the 16th century, / people / in Spain / found this: / Chocolate is good / for people's health. //

Manabu: ⑨ They put sugar / and milk / into the chocolate drink. // ⑩ It tasted good. // ⑪ Then, / an Englishman made the first solid chocolate / around 1850. // (108 words)

🔊 意味のまとまりに注意して，本文全体を音読しよう！

New Words 新出単語の意味を調べよう			
Central America [sèntr(ə)l əmérɪkə]	中央アメリカ	cacao 名 [kəkáu]	1.
Maya [máɪə]	マヤ人	Aztec [ǽztek]	アステカ人
tax 名 [tǽks] B1	2.	Englishman [íŋglɪʃmən] B1	イギリス人
solid 形 [sá(:)ləd] B1	3.	precious 形 [préʃəs] B1	4.

| A | **Comprehension** パラグラフの要点を整理しよう | Fill in the blanks in Japanese. | 【思考力・判断力・表現力】 |

チョコレートの歴史	
3,000年以上前	中央アメリカの人々：初めて（1.　　　　　　　）を食べ，カカオの木を育て始めた。
250年〜900年	マヤ人：カカオ豆を（2.　　　　　　　）として使ったり，神々への行事で使った。
1200年〜1500年	アステカ人：カカオ豆を（3.　　　　　　　）の支払いに使った。
16世紀	スペインの人：チョコレート飲料に砂糖や牛乳を入れるようになった。
1850年頃	あるイギリス人が初めて（4.　　　　　　　）のチョコレートを作った。

| B | **Key Sentences** 重要文について理解しよう | Fill in the blanks and translate the following sentences. | 【知識・技能】【思考力・判断力・表現力】 |

③ **People there started to grow cacao trees.**
（育てることを始める→）育て始める

◆【不定詞】to growは不定詞の名詞用法で，動詞startedの目的語になっている。（→ **Grammar**）

◆ there = 1.＿＿＿＿＿＿＿＿＿＿＿＿＿＿＿＿＿＿＿＿＿

訳：＿＿＿＿＿＿＿＿＿＿＿＿＿＿＿＿＿＿＿＿＿＿＿＿＿＿＿＿＿＿＿＿＿＿

⑤ **They used them in events for the gods, too.**

◆ Theyとthemは別のものを指す。They = the Maya，them = 2.＿＿＿＿＿＿＿＿＿＿＿。

◆ tooは，前文の「お金として使われる」ということに対して「…もまた」という意味で用いられている。

訳：＿＿＿＿＿＿＿＿＿＿＿＿＿＿＿＿＿＿＿＿＿＿＿＿＿＿＿＿＿＿＿＿＿＿

⑦ **From about 1200 to 1500, the Aztecs used cacao beans to pay taxes.**
支払うために

◆【不定詞】to payは不定詞の副詞用法で，「支払うために」という目的を表し，動詞usedを修飾している。

（→ **Grammar**）

訳：＿＿＿＿＿＿＿＿＿＿＿＿＿＿＿＿＿＿＿＿＿＿＿＿＿＿＿＿＿＿＿＿＿＿

⑧ **In the 16th century, people in Spain found this : Chocolate is good for**
　　S　　　　　　　　　V　　　O
　people's health.

◆ ここでのfindは「気づく，わかる，発見する」といった意味である。

◆ thisの具体的な内容はコロン（:）以下の部分である。

訳：＿＿＿＿＿＿＿＿＿＿＿＿＿＿＿＿＿＿＿＿＿＿＿＿＿＿＿＿＿＿＿＿＿＿

＿＿＿＿＿＿＿＿＿＿＿＿＿＿＿＿＿＿＿＿＿＿＿＿＿＿＿＿＿＿＿＿＿＿＿＿

I Was Drinking Chocolate!

Part 3

教科書 p.26-27

🔊 意味のまとまりに注意して，本文全体を聞こう！

Kumi: ①Now, / we want / to hear your questions / about our presentation. //

Takashi: ②What events / did the Maya use cacao beans / for? //

Manabu: ③For their birth, / marriage / and death ceremonies. // ④People offered cacao beans / to the gods. //

Taro: ⑤Is chocolate really good / for our health? // ⑥Can you tell us more / about this? //

Kumi: ⑦People / in Spain / drank chocolate / as a health food. // ⑧Sick people took it / as medicine. // ⑨Um … / any other questions? //

Vivian: ⑩I want / to buy some nice chocolate / for my host mother. // ⑪What do you recommend? //

Kumi: ⑫How about getting 100% cacao chocolate? // ⑬It's not so sweet, / but it's very healthy! // (95 words)

🔊 意味のまとまりに注意して，本文全体を音読しよう！

New Words 新出単語の意味を調べよう		
marriage 名 [mǽrɪdʒ] B1	1.	offer 動 [ɔ́ːfər] A2
recommend 動 [rèkəménd] B1	3.	2.

A Comprehension
パラグラフの要点を整理しよう

Fill in the blanks in Japanese.　　　　【思考力・判断力・表現力】

質疑応答
Q.	マヤ人はどんな行事にカカオ豆を使っていたのか。
A.	誕生，（1.　　　　　　　），死に関する儀式で使っていた。
Q.	チョコレートが健康にいいというのは本当か。
A.	スペインの人々はチョコレートを（2.　　　　　　）として，また，病気の人は（3.　　　　　　）として飲んでいた。
Q.	おすすめのチョコレートはあるか。
A.	カカオ100%のチョコレートはどうか。（4.　　　　　　）ないが，健康的である。

B Key Sentences
重要文について理解しよう

Fill in the blanks and translate the following sentences.
【知識・技能】【思考力・判断力・表現力】

② **What events did the Maya use cacao beans for?**

◆ whatを使った疑問詞疑問文である。what eventsが前置詞forの目的語になっている。

訳：＿＿＿＿＿＿＿＿＿＿＿＿＿＿＿＿＿＿＿＿＿＿＿＿＿＿＿＿＿＿

④ **People offered cacao beans to the gods.**
　　　　S　　　V　　　　O

◆ S＋V＋Oの文である。

◆ offer A to Bで「AをBに差し出す，捧げる」という意味。

訳：＿＿＿＿＿＿＿＿＿＿＿＿＿＿＿＿＿＿＿＿＿＿＿＿＿＿＿＿＿＿

⑧ **Sick people took it as medicine.**

◆ このtakeは「…を飲食する，摂取する」の意味。

◆ it ＝ 1.＿＿＿＿＿＿＿＿＿＿＿＿

訳：＿＿＿＿＿＿＿＿＿＿＿＿＿＿＿＿＿＿＿＿＿＿＿＿＿＿＿＿＿＿

⑫ **How about getting 100% cacao chocolate?**
　　　　　　　　　手に入れること

◆【動名詞】動名詞(動詞の〜ing形)は「〜すること」を表し，名詞の働きをする。この文では動名詞getting が前置詞aboutの目的語になっている。(→ Grammar)

訳：＿＿＿＿＿＿＿＿＿＿＿＿＿＿＿＿＿＿＿＿＿＿＿＿＿＿＿＿＿＿

教科書 p.36-37

🔊 意味のまとまりに注意して，本文全体を聞こう！

1 ①Yuzuru Hanyu started skating / in Sendai / when he was four. // ②At first, / he didn't like practicing, / but he loved showing people / his figure skating skills. // ③He developed his skills / and won international junior competitions / in 2009. //

2 ④After that, / Yuzuru won memorable medals and awards. // ⑤His second Olympic gold / was the 1,000th gold / in the Winter Olympics. // ⑥He was given the People's Honor Award / in 2018. //

3 ⑦Yuzuru faced many hardships / as well. // ⑧After the 2014 Olympics, / he suffered several injuries. // ⑨He even injured his ankle / shortly before the 2018 Olympics. // ⑩However, / he trusted himself / and always thought / about skating. // ⑪Yuzuru thought / that those hardships / gave him the power / to win. // (109 words)

🔊 意味のまとまりに注意して，本文全体を音読しよう！

New Words 新出単語の意味を調べよう			
develop 動 [dɪvéləp] A2	1.	competition 名 [kà(:)mpətíʃ(ə)n] A2	2.
memorable 形 [mém(ə)rəb(ə)l] B1	3.	medal 名 [méd(ə)l] A2	4.
award 名 [əwɔ́:rd] A2	5.	honor 名 [á(:)nər] A2	6.
hardship 名 [há:rdʃìp] B1	7.	suffer 動 [sʌ́fər] B1	8.
injury 名 [ín(d)ʒ(ə)ri] B1	9.	ankle 名 [ǽŋk(ə)l] A2	10.
trust 動 [trʌ́st] A2	11.		

A Comprehension
パラグラフの要点を整理しよう

Fill in the blanks in Japanese.　　　　　　　　　　【思考力・判断力・表現力】

羽生選手の幼少期		
・(1.　　　　　　　)歳のとき，仙台でスケートを始めた。		
・2009年にはジュニアの国際大会で優勝。		
羽生選手の活躍		
功績	・オリンピックで(2.　　　　　　　)を獲得。	
	・2018年に(3.　　　　　　　　　)を受賞。	
羽生選手の苦難		
2014年オリンピック後	けがに苦しんだ。	
2018年オリンピック直前	(4.　　　　　　)を負傷した。	

B Key Sentences
重要文について理解しよう

Fill in the blanks and translate the following sentences.

【知識・技能】【思考力・判断力・表現力】

② **At first, he didn't like practicing, but he loved showing people his figure skating skills.**
　　　　　　　　　　　　　　　練習すること　　　　　　　　　　　見せること

◆ practicing と showing は動名詞。practicing は didn't like の目的語，showing は loved の目的語になっている。

訳：..

⑤ **His second Olympic gold was the 1,000th gold in the Winter Olympics.**
　　　　　　S　　　　　　　　　V　　　　　　　　　　　　　　C

◆ S＋V＋C の文。「S＝C（S は C である）」の関係になっている。

◆ gold とは，gold 1._____ のこと。

訳：..

⑦ **Yuzuru faced many hardships as well.**

◆ この face は「(困難など)に直面する」の意味の動詞。

訳：..

⑪ **Yuzuru thought that those hardships gave him the power to win.**
　　S　　　　V　　　　　　　　　　　　　　　　O

◆【S＋V＋O（＝that-節）】that 以下全体が thought の目的語になっている。（→ **Grammar**）

◆ that-節中は S＋V＋O₁＋O₂ の構造になっている。

　　S：those hardships, V：2._____ , O₁：him, O₂：3._____

訳：..

Inspiration on the Ice

Part 2

教科書 p.38-39

🔊 意味のまとまりに注意して，本文全体を聞こう！

1 ①The Great East Japan Earthquake / in 2011 / was another hardship / for Yuzuru. // ②He was training / at his home rink / at the time. // ③Yuzuru escaped / from the arena. // ④Ten days later, / he started skating again / with the help of people / around him. //

2 ⑤Since then, / Yuzuru has thought about people / in disaster areas. // ⑥He has skated / in a lot of charity ice shows. // ⑦When he won his first Olympic gold, / he said, / "I'm here / because many people / around the world / have supported me." //

3 ⑧After the 2018 Olympics, / Yuzuru paraded / through the streets of Sendai. // ⑨About 100,000 people / welcomed him. // ⑩"I'm happy / to come back here / with this gold medal," / Yuzuru said / during the ceremony. // (112 words)

🔊 意味のまとまりに注意して，本文全体を音読しよう！

New Words 新出単語の意味を調べよう

rink 名 [ríŋk]	1.	escape 動 [ɪskéɪp] B1	2.
arena 名 [ərí:nə] B2	3.	disaster 名 [dɪzǽstər] B1	4.
parade 動 [pəréɪd]	5.		

A Comprehension
パラグラフの要点を整理しよう

Fill in the blanks in Japanese.

【思考力・判断力・表現力】

さらなる苦難	
東日本大震災	・本拠地のリンクでの練習中に地震発生。競技場から(1.　　　　　　　)。 ・(2.　　　　　　　)後，周囲の人のおかげで練習を再開。
被災地の人々への思い	
・慈善活動：数多くのアイスショーに出演。 ・最初の(3.　　　　　　　)を獲得。 ➡感謝の言葉：「今ここにいるのは世界中の人たちの支援のおかげ。」	
仙台でのパレード	
・約(4.　　　　　　　)人が歓迎。 ➡喜びの言葉：「金メダルを持って仙台に帰って来られてうれしい。」	

B Key Sentences
重要文について理解しよう

Fill in the blanks and translate the following sentences.

【知識・技能】【思考力・判断力・表現力】

④ Ten days later, he started skating again with the help of people around him.
　　　　　　　　　S　　started　skating　　　　　　　O

◆ 動名詞 1.＿＿＿＿＿＿＿＿＿＿ が動詞 started の目的語になっている。

訳：

⑤ Since then, Yuzuru has thought about people in disaster areas.

◆【現在完了形】has thought は「(その時以来)ずっと思っている」という状態の継続を表す。(→ Grammar)

訳：

⑦ When he won his first Olympic gold, he said, "I'm here because many
　　　　　　　　　　　　　　　　　S　said　　　　　　　　　　O

people around the world have supported me."

◆ because-節中の主語は many people around the world，動詞は have supported である。

◆【現在完了形】have supported は「ずっと支えてきてくれた」という状態の継続を表す。(→ Grammar)

訳：

⑩ "I'm happy to come back here with this gold medal," Yuzuru said during
　　　　　　　　　　　　O　　　　　　　　　　　　　　　　　　S　　V

the ceremony.

◆ 発言内容(" "の部分)が動詞 2.＿＿＿＿＿＿＿＿＿＿ の目的語になっている。

訳：

🔊 意味のまとまりに注意して，本文全体を聞こう！

Reporter: ① I'd like to ask you / about your friendship / with Javier Fernandez. //

Yuzuru: ② Thank you. // ③ I'm glad / to talk about Javier / because I know / he is often asked / about me / by Japanese reporters. //

Reporter: ④ What's he like? //

Yuzuru: ⑤ He's very kind. // ⑥ Too kind / to compete, / I think. // ⑦ I won the gold medal / at the Olympics, / and he took third place. // ⑧ I wept. // ⑨ We trained together, / and I knew / he worked hard / to get a medal. // ⑩ I was proud / of him. //

Reporter: ⑪ What does he mean / to you? //

Yuzuru: ⑫ He means a lot / to me. // ⑬ We've always inspired / each other. // ⑭ I got the gold / because he's been / with me. // (102 words)

🔊 意味のまとまりに注意して，本文全体を音読しよう！

New Words 新出単語の意味を調べよう			
Javier Fernandez [hɑ:vjéər fə(:)nǽndez]	ハビエル・フェルナンデス	compete 動 [kəmpíːt] B1	1.
wept 動 [wépt]	2. の過去形・過去分詞形	weep 動 [wíːp]	3.
proud 形 [prάud] B1	4.	inspire 動 [ɪnspάɪər] B1	5.

A Comprehension
パラグラフの要点を整理しよう

Fill in the blanks in Japanese.　　【思考力・判断力・表現力】

羽生選手へのインタビュー：フェルナンデス選手との(1.　　　　　　　)について	
Q.	フェルナンデス選手はどんな人か。
A.	・とてもやさしい。 ・メダルを取るために一生懸命練習しているのを知っていたので，フェルナンデス選手がオリンピックで(2.　　　　　　)になったとき，涙が出た。
Q.	羽生選手にとってフェルナンデス選手とは。
A.	・お互いに常に(3.　　　　　　)し合っている。 ・フェルナンデス選手がいっしょだったから(4.　　　　　　)が取れた。

B Key Sentences
重要文について理解しよう

Fill in the blanks and translate the following sentences.

【知識・技能】【思考力・判断力・表現力】

③ **I'm glad to talk about Javier because I know he is often asked about me by Japanese reporters.**

◆ because以下が理由を表す節になっている。

◆【受け身】is askedは受け身で，「たずねられる」という意味。この文では副詞oftenが挿入されている。

(→ Grammar)

訳 :

⑥ **Too kind to compete, I think.**

◆ 省略を補い，通常の語順にすると，I think that 1.＿＿＿＿＿＿＿＿＿ too kind to compete. となる。

◆ too ... to ～は，「～するには…すぎる」という意味。

訳 :

⑨ **We trained together, and I knew he worked hard to get a medal.**

◆ Weは具体的には，羽生選手と(2.　　　　　　)選手のこと。heは(3.　　　　　　)選手のこと。

◆ to getは不定詞の副詞用法で，「～するために」(目的)を表す。

訳 :

⑭ **I got the gold because he's been with me.**

◆ he's been ＝ he 4.＿＿＿＿＿＿ been

訳 :

Esports' Time Has Arrived

Part 1

教科書 p.50-51

◀)) 意味のまとまりに注意して，本文全体を聞こう！

1 ① There is a popular, new sport / today: / esports. // ② Esports is the short name / for "electronic sports." // ③ Esports players play video games / in individual / or team competitions. //

2 ④ In the late 20th century, / people started playing video games / for fun. // ⑤ Today, / many people enjoy them / in a different way. // ⑥ Computers and other machines today / are smarter and cheaper / than those of the 20th century. // ⑦ Also, / Internet technology has advanced, / so people can now compete online / with gamers / around the world. // ⑧ They often use their own powerful machines. //

3 ⑨ Many players have become very skilled, / and even professional players / have appeared. // ⑩ Many organizations have started tournaments. // ⑪ As a result, / such video gaming has gotten the name / "esports." // (113 words)

◀)) 意味のまとまりに注意して，本文全体を音読しよう！

New Words 新出単語の意味を調べよう			
esports 名 [íːspɔ̀ːrts]	1.	electronic 形 [ɪlèktrá(ː)nɪk] B1	2.
individual 形 [ìndɪvídʒu(ə)l] B1	3.	advance 動 [ədvǽns] B1	4.
gamer 名 [géɪmər]	5.	skilled 形 [skíld] B2	6.
organization 名 [ɔ̀ːrɡ(ə)nəzéɪʃ(ə)n] B1	7.	gaming 名 [géɪmɪŋ]	8.

A Comprehension パラグラフの要点を整理しよう　Fill in the blanks in Japanese. 【思考力・判断力・表現力】

eスポーツ … 個人，またはチームで，テレビゲームで競う新しいスポーツ	
20世紀後半 ↓ 現在	・人々は(1.　　　　　　　)のためにテレビゲームをするようになった。 ・技術の進歩により，世界中の人々とオンラインで(2.　　　　　　)できるようになった。 ・熟練したプレーヤーや(3.　　　　　　)のプレーヤーも現れた。 ・(4.　　　　　　)も開催されている。

B Key Sentences 重要文について理解しよう　Fill in the blanks and translate the following sentences.

【知識・技能】【思考力・判断力・表現力】

④ In the late 20th century, people <u>started</u> <u>playing video games</u> for fun.
　　　　　　　　　　　　　　　　　　　S　　　V　　　　　　O

◆ start ～ingで「(～することを始める→)～し始める」という意味。

訳：_____

⑥ Computers and other machines today are smarter and cheaper than those of the 20th century.

◆【比較(比較級)】A ... 比較級＋than Bで「AはBよりも～」を表す。ここではComputers and other machines todayとthose of the 20th centuryが比較されている。(→ **Grammar**)

◆ thoseは直前の複数名詞を指す。ここでは，those = 1._____

_____ 。

訳：_____

_____

⑦ Also, Internet technology has advanced, so people can now compete online with gamers around the world.

◆ has advancedは完了を表す現在完了形。

◆ この文のonlineは「オンライン上で」を意味する副詞で，動詞competeを修飾している。

訳：_____

_____

⑪ As a result, <u>such video gaming</u> <u>has gotten</u> the name "esports."
　　　　　　　　　　　S　　　　　　　　　V　　　　　O

◆ the nameと"esports"は同格の関係であり，「『eスポーツ』という名前」という意味になる。

訳：_____

Esports' Time Has Arrived

🔊 意味のまとまりに注意して，本文全体を聞こう！

1 ①Esports tournaments now take place / online / or in big arenas / all over the world. // ②Players compete / against each other / in various games, / such as battle games, / card games / and sports games. //

2 ③Becoming a great esports player / is often as difficult / as becoming a great player / of any other kind of sport. // ④For example, / players need / to respond quickly / and think hard / about strategies. // ⑤They also need good communication skills / because they often work / as a team. //

3 ⑥Today / in Japan, / more and more people believe / that esports will change society. // ⑦Some high schools have special programs / for esports. // ⑧The students there / learn the basics / of IT / and practice / how to win games. //

(111 words)　🔊 意味のまとまりに注意して，本文全体を音読しよう！

New Words 新出単語の意味を調べよう			
battle 名 [bǽt(ə)l] B1	1.	respond 動 [rɪspá(:)nd] B1	2.
strategy 名 [strǽtədʒi] A2	3.	society 名 [səsáɪəti] A2	4.
basic 名 [béɪsɪk] A2	5.		

A Comprehension パラグラフの要点を整理しよう　Fill in the blanks in Japanese.　【思考力・判断力・表現力】

eスポーツの現在
・世界中でオンラインや大きな競技場でトーナメントが開催されている。
・戦闘ゲーム，カードゲーム，（1.　　　　　　）ゲームなど，さまざまなゲームで競う。

すぐれたeスポーツ選手になるために
・すばやく反応したり，（2.　　　　　　）を考えたりする必要がある。
・（3.　　　　　　　　）スキルも必要である。

日本におけるeスポーツ
・eスポーツのための特別プログラムがある高校がある。
→（4.　　　　　　）の基礎やゲームの勝ち方を学ぶ。

B Key Sentences 重要文について理解しよう　Fill in the blanks and translate the following sentences.

【知識・技能】【思考力・判断力・表現力】

① **Esports tournaments now take place online or in big arenas all over the world.**

◆ online と in big arenas all over the world が or によって並列に結ばれている。

訳：

③ **Becoming a great esports player is often as difficult as becoming a great player of any other kind of sport.**

◆【比較（原級）】A ... as ＋原級＋as B で「AはBと同じくらい〜である」を表す。ここでは Becoming a great esports player と becoming a great player of any other kind of sport が比較されている。2つの becoming はどちらも動名詞で，「…になること」という意味である。（→ Grammar）

訳：

⑥ **Today in Japan, more and more people believe that esports will change society.**

S　　　　　　　V　　　　　O

◆ S＋V＋O（＝that-節）の文。more and more ...は「ますます多くの…」という意味。

訳：

⑧ **The students there learn the basics of IT and practice how to win games.**

V₁　　　　　　　　　　　　V₂

◆ 動詞 1.　　　　　　　と 2.　　　　　　　は and によって並列に結ばれている。

訳：

Esports' Time Has Arrived

Part 3

教科書 p.56-57

🔊 意味のまとまりに注意して，本文全体を聞こう！

①I'm 15. // ②I love esports. // ③I hope / to become a good esports player. // ④It's my future dream. // ⑤But my parents don't want me / to become an esports player. // ⑥They say / playing computer games / is only a waste / of time. // ⑦Am I wrong? //

Answer //

⑧I live / in South Korea. // ⑨I'm working hard / to become a professional esports player. // ⑩You have the same dream, / too, / right? // ⑪Then, / learn the following things. //

⑫1. Be strong and healthy / —— physically and mentally. //

⑬2. Improve your language skills / —— especially English skills. //

⑭3. Cultivate your spirit / of fair play. //

⑮I know / these are not easy. // ⑯But / if you work hard, / your parents will understand you. // (107 words)   🔊 意味のまとまりに注意して，本文全体を音読しよう！

New Words 新出単語の意味を調べよう		
physically 副 [fízɪk(ə)li] A2	1.	mentally 副 [mént(ə)li] B1	2.
cultivate 動 [kʌ́ltɪvèɪt] B1	3.		

A Comprehension
パラグラフの要点を整理しよう

Fill in the blanks in Japanese.

【思考力・判断力・表現力】

Q&Aサイト		
質問者	悩み：eスポーツ選手になりたいが，（1.　　　　　　）が反対している。	
	・eスポーツ選手になるのが将来の夢。	
	・両親は，コンピュータゲームをするのは（2.　　　　　　）の無駄だと言う。	
回答者	回答：以下のことを身につけるとよい。	
	①身体的にも精神的にも強く（3.　　　　　）であること	
	②言語のスキルを（4.　　　　　）させること	
	③フェアプレーの精神を養うこと	

B Key Sentences
重要文について理解しよう

Fill in the blanks and translate the following sentences.

【知識・技能】【思考力・判断力・表現力】

⑤ But <u>my parents</u> <u>don't want</u> <u>me</u> <u>to become</u> an esports player.
　　　　　S　　　　　　V　　　　O　　to-不定詞

◆【S＋V＋O＋to-不定詞】don't want me to ～は「私に～してほしくない」という意味になる。

(→ **Grammar**)

訳：_____

⑥ <u>They</u> <u>say</u> <u>playing computer games is only a waste of time.</u>
　　S　　V　　　　　　　　　　　O

◆ They = 1._____

◆ say と playing の間には 2._____ が省略されている。

訳：_____

⑨ I'm working hard to become a professional esports player.

◆ am working は現在進行形であり，今現在「努力している」ことを表している。

◆ to become は目的を表す不定詞の副詞用法で，動詞句 am working hard を修飾している。

訳：_____

⑯ But if you work hard, your parents will understand you.

◆ if-節は条件を表す副詞節であり，「もし…なら」という意味。

訳：_____

🔊 意味のまとまりに注意して，本文全体を聞こう！

Kumi: ①Look at this poster, / Vivian. //

Vivian: ②Hmm … // ③The man / wearing a mask / is dancing, / and the two men are playing music. //

Kumi: ④Yeah. // ⑤This poster was for a *Kyogen* performance / in France. //

Vivian: ⑥I see. // ⑦Then, / who are Mansaku, / Mansai, / and Yuki Nomura? //

Kumi: ⑧They are famous *Kyogen* performers. // ⑨Actually, / they are a grandfather, / a father, / and a son. //

Vivian: ⑩Do you think / I'll like watching *Kyogen*? // ⑪The stories seem difficult / for me. //

Kumi: ⑫Don't worry! // ⑬The stories are simple and funny. // ⑭In addition, / *Kyogen* has a traditional and beautiful style, / just like *No*, / *Kabuki*, / and *Bunraku*. //

Vivian: ⑮Okay. // ⑯Now, / I want / to learn more / about *Kyogen*. //

Kumi: ⑰Awesome! // ⑱Let's go / to the theater / sometime. //

Vivian: ⑲I can't wait! // (110 words)　🔊 意味のまとまりに注意して，本文全体を音読しよう！

New Words 新出単語の意味を調べよう			
theatrical 形 [θiǽtrɪk(ə)l]	1.	hmm 間 [m]	うーん
seem 動 [síːm] A2	2.	awesome 形 [ɔ́ːs(ə)m] B1	3.
sometime 副 [sʌ́mtàɪm] B1	4.		

A Comprehension
パラグラフの要点を整理しよう

Fill in the blanks in Japanese.

【思考力・判断力・表現力】

久美とヴィヴィアンの会話

・（1.　　　　　　　）で行われた狂言のポスター

　…面をつけて踊っている男性と，音楽を演奏している男性たち。

・野村万作さん，萬斎さん，裕基さんは有名な（2.　　　　　　　）で，祖父・父・息子である。

・狂言のストーリーは（3.　　　　　　）でおもしろい。さらに，（4.　　　　　　）的で美しい型が
ある。

・ヴィヴィアンは狂言についてもっと知りたいと思っている。

B Key Sentences
重要文について理解しよう

Fill in the blanks and translate the following sentences.

【知識・技能】【思考力・判断力・表現力】

③ **The man wearing a mask is dancing, and the two men are playing music.**

　◆【現在分詞】wearing a mask が後ろから the man を修飾している。（→ **Grammar**）

　◆ and によって2つの節がつながれている。前半の節では，the man wearing a mask が主語，1.＿＿＿＿＿
　＿＿＿＿＿＿＿＿＿＿＿＿＿＿ が動詞になっている。

　訳 : ＿＿＿＿＿＿＿＿＿＿＿＿＿＿＿＿＿＿＿＿＿＿＿＿＿＿＿＿＿＿＿＿＿＿＿＿＿＿＿

⑪ **The stories seem difficult for me.**
　　　　S　　　V　　C

　◆ S＋V＋Cの文。「S＝C」，つまり「(狂言の)ストーリー＝難しい」という関係になっている。

　訳 : ＿＿＿＿＿＿＿＿＿＿＿＿＿＿＿＿＿＿＿＿＿＿＿＿＿＿＿＿＿＿＿＿＿＿＿＿＿＿＿

⑭ **In addition, _Kyogen_ has a traditional and beautiful style, just like _No_,**
　　　　　　　　　　　　　　　　　　　　　　　　　　　　　　　　　　　　A

　Kabuki, and _Bunraku_.
　　　B　　　　　C

　◆ A, B, and C という形で3つの具体例がつながれている。

　訳 : ＿＿＿＿＿＿＿＿＿＿＿＿＿＿＿＿＿＿＿＿＿＿＿＿＿＿＿＿＿＿＿＿＿＿＿＿＿＿＿

⑯ **Now, I want to learn more about _Kyogen_.**

　◆ want to ～で「～したい」という意味。to learn は不定詞の名詞用法。

　◆ more の品詞は（2.　　　　　　　）で，「もっと多くのこと」という意味。他動詞 learn の目的語になっている。

　訳 : ＿＿＿＿＿＿＿＿＿＿＿＿＿＿＿＿＿＿＿＿＿＿＿＿＿＿＿＿＿＿＿＿＿＿＿＿＿＿＿

🔊 意味のまとまりに注意して，本文全体を聞こう！

1 ①Mansai was born / in 1966. // ②His family has performed *Kyogen* / since the Edo period. // ③Both his father and grandfather / are living national treasures. // ④Mansai performed / on stage / for the first time / at the age of three. //

2 ⑤*Kyogen* is a traditional art / passed down / from one generation to another. // ⑥*Kyogen* performers go through severe training / to learn the tradition. // ⑦However, / just being strict / in traditional ways / may not make *Kyogen* better. //

3 ⑧Mansai believes / he can perform *Kyogen* better / by doing different things. // ⑨For example, / he studied Shakespeare's plays / in London / in 1994. // ⑩He also acts / in movies / and appears / on TV. // ⑪He even advised Yuzuru Hanyu / on his skating program, / *SEIMEI*. // ⑫In this way, / Mansai has drawn people's attention / to *Kyogen*. // (120 words)　🔊 意味のまとまりに注意して，本文全体を音読しよう！

New Words 新出単語の意味を調べよう			
living 形 [lívɪŋ] A1	1.	generation 名 [dʒènəréɪʃ(ə)n] A2	2.
severe 形 [sɪvíər] B1	3.	Shakespeare [ʃéɪkspɪər]	シェイクスピア
advise 動 [ədváɪz] A2	4.		

A Comprehension
パラグラフの要点を整理しよう

Fill in the blanks in Japanese.

【思考力・判断力・表現力】

野村萬斎さんについて		
生い立ち	・1966年生まれ。3歳のときに狂言の初舞台を踏む。 ・野村家は江戸時代から狂言を演じており，父と祖父は(1.　　　　　)である。	
狂言の継承	・狂言：代々受け継がれてきた伝統芸能。 ・狂言師は(2.　　　　　)を学ぶために厳しい訓練を積む。	
活動	・ロンドンで(3.　　　　　)の演劇を勉強。 ・(4.　　　　　)やテレビに出演。 ・『SEIMEI』の演目で羽生結弦選手に助言。	→ 狂言に人々の注目を集める。

B Key Sentences
重要文について理解しよう

Fill in the blanks and translate the following sentences.

【知識・技能】【思考力・判断力・表現力】

② **His family has performed *Kyogen* since the Edo period.**

◆ has performedは「(ずっと)演じてきた」という継続を表す現在完了形。sinceは「…以来」の意味。

訳：_____

⑤ ***Kyogen* is a traditional art passed down from one generation to another.**
　　　S　 V　　　C

◆【過去分詞】passed down以下が後ろからa traditional artを修飾している。(→ **Grammar**)

訳：_____

⑦ **However, just being strict in traditional ways may not make *Kyogen* better.**
　　　　　　　　S　　　　　　　　　　　　　　 V　　　 O
　　　　　　　　　　　　　　　　　　　　　　　　　　C

◆ S＋V＋O＋Cの文。make＋O＋Cは「OをCにする」という意味。「O＝C」, つまり「狂言＝よりよい」という関係になっている。

◆ 文の主語は動名詞 1._____ からなる名詞句。

訳：_____

⑪ **He even advised Yuzuru Hanyu on his skating program, *SEIMEI*.**

◆ 2._____ と*SEIMEI*は同格の関係であり，「彼のスケート演目である『SEIMEI』」という意味。

訳：_____

Mansai, *Kyogen* Performer

Part 3

教科書 p.70-71

🔊 意味のまとまりに注意して，本文全体を聞こう！

1 ①One of Mansai's new efforts / involved digital technology. // ②He performed / as a motion capture actor / for the movie / *Shin Godzilla* / in 2016. // ③It was easy / for Mansai / to play the role / of Godzilla. // ④He moved / in the *Kyogen* style! // ⑤"I'm glad / that *Kyogen*'s history / of more than 650 years / is mixed / with the DNA / of Godzilla," / Mansai said. //

2 ⑥Mansai was chosen / as the adviser / of the opening and closing ceremonies / of the Tokyo Olympics and Paralympics. // ⑦This was / because he worked / on the fusion / of classical art and modern theater. // ⑧Mansai's goal is / to become a bridge / to pass on the traditional art / to the next generation. // (107 words)

🔊 意味のまとまりに注意して，本文全体を音読しよう！

New Words 新出単語の意味を調べよう			
involve 動 [ɪnvá(:)lv] B1	1.	digital 形 [dídʒɪt(ə)l] B1	2.
motion 名 [móuʃ(ə)n] B2	3.	capture 名 [kǽptʃər] B1	4.
Godzilla [gɑdzílə]	ゴジラ	adviser 名 [ədváɪzər] B1	5.
fusion 名 [fjúːʒ(ə)n]	6.	classical 形 [klǽsɪk(ə)l] B1	7.
modern 形 [mɑ́(:)dərn] A2	8.		

A **Comprehension**
パラグラフの要点を整理しよう

Fill in the blanks in Japanese.

【思考力・判断力・表現力】

萬斎さんの新たな努力
①2016年，映画『シン・ゴジラ』でモーションアクターを務め，狂言の型でゴジラの動きを演じた。 　→狂言の歴史とゴジラの(1.　　　　　　　)が混ざり合ったことに喜びを感じる。
②古典芸能と近代演劇の(2.　　　　　　)に取り組んだ。 　→東京オリンピック・パラリンピックの(3.　　　　　　　)のアドバイザーに選ばれた。
➡萬斎さんの目標：伝統芸能を次世代に伝える(4.　　　　　　)となること

B **Key Sentences**
重要文について理解しよう

Fill in the blanks and translate the following sentences.

【知識・技能】【思考力・判断力・表現力】

③ <u>It</u> was easy <u>for Mansai</u> to play the role of Godzilla.

◆【It is ... (for A) to 〜】to以下の内容を形式主語itで表している。to play ...の意味上の主語は 1._____ である。(→ **Grammar**)

訳：_____

⑤ "I'm glad that *Kyogen*'s history of more than 650 years is mixed with the DNA of Godzilla," Mansai said.

◆ that-節の中は *Kyogen*'s history of more than 650 years が主語で，受け身の 2._____ が動詞である。

訳：_____

_____

⑦ This was because he worked on the fusion of classical art and modern theater.

◆ This was because ＋ S ＋ V で「これはSがVだからであった」という意味。

訳：_____

⑧ <u>Mansai's goal</u> <u>is</u> <u>to become a bridge (to pass on the traditional art to the</u>
　　　S　　　　　　V　　C

<u>next generation)</u>.

◆ S＋V＋Cの文。「S＝C (SはCである)」の関係であり，to become以下全体がCになっている。

◆ to becomeは不定詞の名詞用法(「〜すること」)。to passは不定詞の形容詞用法(「〜する(ための)」)で，a bridgeを後ろから修飾している。

訳：_____

In this Corner of the World

Part 1

教科書 p.78-79

🔊 意味のまとまりに注意して，本文全体を聞こう！

1 ①A lot of people helped / to make the movie / *In this Corner of the World*. // ②When the movie project started, / there was not enough money. // ③The production staff asked people / to donate money / on the Internet. // ④Surprisingly, / the staff gathered about 40 million yen / from more than 3,000 people. //

2 ⑤The movie became a hit. // ⑥One of the reasons / for this / was the power / of social media. // ⑦Good reviews spread, / and more and more people went / to see it. //

3 ⑧Another reason was / that the movie shows the real life / of a family / during World War II. // ⑨The family members led quite an ordinary life, / just as we do. // ⑩That appealed strongly / to a lot of people. // ⑪Ever since the movie came out, / it has been attracting many viewers. // (127 words)

🔊 意味のまとまりに注意して，本文全体を音読しよう！

New Words 新出単語の意味を調べよう			
production 名 [prədʌkʃ(ə)n] A2	1.	staff 名 [stæf] A2	2.
donate 動 [dóuneɪt] B2	3.	ordinary 形 [ɔ́:rd(ə)nèri] B1	4.
appeal 動 [əpí:l] B2	5.	attract 動 [ətrǽkt] B1	6.
viewer 名 [vjú:ər] B2	7.		

A Comprehension
パラグラフの要点を整理しよう

Fill in the blanks in Japanese.

【思考力・判断力・表現力】

映画『この世界の片隅に』	
制作まで	プロジェクト開始時の問題点：資金不足 →(1.　　　　　)上で人々に寄付を募り，3,000人以上から約(2.　　　　　)円集まった。
公開後	ヒットした。 理由①：(3.　　　　　)の力 　　…よい評価が拡散され，ますます多くの人が見に行った。 理由②：第二次世界大戦中の(4.　　　　　)を描いていたから 　　…戦時中の人々も自分たちと同じようにごくふつうの生活を送っていたという点が，多くの人々の心に訴えた。

B Key Sentences
重要文について理解しよう

Fill in the blanks and translate the following sentences.

【知識・技能】【思考力・判断力・表現力】

③ <u>The production staff</u> <u>asked</u> <u>people</u> <u>to donate</u> money on the Internet.
　　　　　　S　　　　　　　V　　　O　　　to-不定詞

◆ S＋V＋O＋to-不定詞の文。Oはto-不定詞以下の意味上の主語である。

訳：＿＿＿＿＿＿＿＿＿＿＿＿＿＿＿＿＿＿＿＿＿＿＿＿＿＿＿＿＿＿

⑥ <u>One of the reasons for this</u> <u>was</u> <u>the power of social media.</u>
　　　　　　　S　　　　　　　　　V　　　　　　C

◆ S＋V＋Cの文。「S＝C」の関係になっている。

◆ thisとは，映画が(1.　　　　　　　　　　　　　)ことを指している。

訳：＿＿＿＿＿＿＿＿＿＿＿＿＿＿＿＿＿＿＿＿＿＿＿＿＿＿＿＿＿＿

⑨ The family members led quite an ordinary life, just as we do.

◆ just as＋S＋Vで「ちょうどSがVするのと同じように」の意味。このasの品詞は(2.　　　　　　　)。

訳：＿＿＿＿＿＿＿＿＿＿＿＿＿＿＿＿＿＿＿＿＿＿＿＿＿＿＿＿＿＿

⑪ Ever since the movie came out, it has been attracting many viewers.

◆【現在完了進行形】has been attractingは現在完了進行形で，「（ずっと）魅了し（続け）ている」という意味。ever since ...は「…以来ずっと」という意味で，動作の起点を表す。（→ Grammar）

訳：＿＿＿＿＿＿＿＿＿＿＿＿＿＿＿＿＿＿＿＿＿＿＿＿＿＿＿＿＿＿

🔊 意味のまとまりに注意して，本文全体を聞こう！

1 ①The main character Suzu / gets married / to Shusaku / and moves / from Hiroshima / to Kure. // ②She tries hard / to get used to the new environment. //

2 ③As time passes, / people are running short of food. // ④Suzu cooks meals / by using wild plants. // ⑤One day, / when she cooks, / she uses a method / that was invented / by a famous samurai / and increases the amount / of food. //

3 ⑥Suzu likes drawing pictures. // ⑦One day, / when she draws a picture / of battleships / on a hill, / the military police suspect her / of spying. // ⑧They search her house / for some signs / of spying. // ⑨The people / in her family / try hard / not to laugh / because Suzu is so absent-minded / that she can never spy! // ⑩They burst into laughter / after the police leave. // (122 words)

🔊 意味のまとまりに注意して，本文全体を音読しよう！

New Words 新出単語の意味を調べよう			
marry 動 [mǽri] A2	1.	method 名 [méθəd] A2	2.
invent 動 [ɪnvént] A2	3.	amount 名 [əmáʊnt] B1	4.
battleship 名 [bǽt(ə)lʃìp]	5.	military 形 [mílətèri] A2	6.
suspect 動 [səspékt] B2	7.	search 動 [sə́ːrtʃ] B1	8.
absent-minded 形 [æbs(ə)ntmáɪndɪd]	9.	burst 動 [bə́ːrst] B1	10.
laughter 名 [lǽftər] B1	11.		

A Comprehension
パラグラフの要点を整理しよう

Fill in the blanks in Japanese.

【思考力・判断力・表現力】

主人公すずの暮らし
▶周作と結婚し，広島から呉に引っ越した。
▶戦時下で，食料が(1.　　　　　)するようになっていった。 　→すずは(2.　　　　　)を使って食事を作った。
▶ある日，すずが軍艦の絵を描いていると，憲兵に(3.　　　　　)の容疑をかけられた。 　→ぼんやりした性格のすずがスパイなんてできるはずがないと知っている家族は必死に 　(4.　　　　　)をこらえた。

B Key Sentences
重要文について理解しよう

Fill in the blanks and translate the following sentences.

【知識・技能】【思考力・判断力・表現力】

③ **As time passes, people are running short of food.**

◆ このasは「…につれて」という比例の意味を表す接続詞。

訳：＿＿＿＿＿＿＿＿＿＿＿＿＿＿＿＿＿＿＿＿＿＿＿＿＿＿＿

⑤ **One day, when she cooks, she uses a method that was invented by a famous**
　　　　　　　　　　　　　　　　　　　　　　　　　関係代名詞
samurai and increases the amount of food.

◆ 主節中では，2つの動詞usesと 1.＿＿＿＿＿＿＿ がandによって並列に結ばれている。

◆【関係代名詞(主格)】thatは主格の関係代名詞で, that以下の節全体が先行詞a methodを修飾している。

（→ Grammar）

訳：＿＿＿＿＿＿＿＿＿＿＿＿＿＿＿＿＿＿＿＿＿＿＿＿＿＿＿

⑧ **They search her house for some signs of spying.**
　　S　　V　　　O

◆ S＋V＋Oの文である。for ...は「…を求めて」の意味。

◆ They ＝ 2.＿＿＿＿＿＿＿＿＿＿＿＿＿＿＿ , her ＝ Suzu's である。

訳：＿＿＿＿＿＿＿＿＿＿＿＿＿＿＿＿＿＿＿＿＿＿＿＿＿＿＿

⑨ **The people in her family try hard not to laugh because Suzu is so absent-**
minded that she can never spy!

◆ not to laughはto-不定詞の否定形で，「〜しないように」という意味。

◆ so＋形容詞＋that＋S＋Vの形で「とても…(形容詞)なのでSはVする」の意味になる。

訳：＿＿＿＿＿＿＿＿＿＿＿＿＿＿＿＿＿＿＿＿＿＿＿＿＿＿＿
　＿＿＿＿＿＿＿＿＿＿＿＿＿＿＿＿＿＿＿＿＿＿＿＿＿＿＿

🔊 意味のまとまりに注意して，本文全体を聞こう！

①Shusaku asks Suzu / to come / to his office / with a notebook / which he forgot. // ②Actually, / he wants / to talk / with her. // ③On a bridge, / they are having a chat / about their fateful meeting / and married life. //

Suzu: ④I guess / I'm just afraid / I'll wake up / from a dream. //

Shusaku: ⑤Dream? //

Suzu: ⑥Having to change my name / and move somewhere new / was hard / for me, / but you've been so kind, / and I've made friends. // ⑦I don't want / to wake up / because I'm really happy / to be who I am today. //

Shusaku: ⑧I see. // ⑨The past and the paths / we did not choose, / I guess, / are really like a dream, / if you think / about it. // ⑩Suzu, / choosing to marry you / was the best decision / of my life. // (121 words)

🔊 意味のまとまりに注意して，本文全体を音読しよう！

New Words 新出単語の意味を調べよう

chat 名 [tʃǽt] B1	1.	fateful 形 [féɪtʃ(ə)l]	2.
somewhere 副 [sʌ́mwèər] A2	3.	path 名 [pǽθ] A2	4.

 **A Comprehension**
パラグラフの要点を整理しよう
Fill in the blanks in Japanese. 【思考力・判断力・表現力】

映画のワンシーン	
▶すずと周作が(1.　　　　　)の上で話している場面。2人の出会いや結婚生活について話している。	
すず	・名前が変わることや新しい場所に引っ越すことは大変だったが，周作はやさしく，(2.　　　　　)もできて，今がとても幸せである。 →(3.　　　　　)から覚めてしまうのではないかと不安。
周作	・過去のことや自分たちが選ばなかった道は夢のようなものだ。 ・人生における最良の決断は，すずと(4.　　　　　)したことである。

B Key Sentences
重要文について理解しよう
Fill in the blanks and translate the following sentences.
【知識・技能】【思考力・判断力・表現力】

① Shusaku asks Suzu to come to his office with ⎡a notebook⎤ which he forgot.

◆【関係代名詞（目的格）】which は目的格の関係代名詞で，which 以下の節が先行詞 a notebook を修飾している。(→ **Grammar**)

訳：_____

⑥ Having to change my name and move somewhere new was hard for me, / but you've been so kind, / and I've made friends.

◆ Having to ～は have to ～（～しなければならない）の動名詞形で，主語になっている。
◆ but と and で 3 つの節がつながれている。1 つ目の節の主語は Having から 1._____ まで。

訳：_____

⑦ I don't want to wake up because I'm really happy to be who I am today.

◆ who I am today は「現在の私」という意味で，be の補語になっている。

訳：_____

⑨ The past and ⎡the paths⎤ we did not choose, I guess, are really like a dream, if you think about it.

◆ we did not choose は the paths を修飾している。the paths の後には目的格の関係代名詞 2._____ が省略されている。
◆ I guess は挿入句として文中に挿入されている。通常であれば，I guess (that) ...と文頭にくる。

訳：_____

Part 3 page 39

🔊)) 意味のまとまりに注意して，本文全体を聞こう！

1 ①Gradually, / the situation gets worse. // ②Suzu and her niece / experience an air raid. // ③When they are walking / hand in hand / after the raid, / an unexploded bomb explodes. // ④Her niece is killed / and Suzu loses her right hand. //

2 ⑤About four months after the war ends, / Suzu finds / "the new bomb" has taken the lives / of her mother and father. // ⑥Her younger sister / is ill in bed. // ⑦She has lost people / she loves. //

3 ⑧Through the movie, / we can find out / how people lived / during the war. // ⑨They led ordinary lives. // ⑩They shared time / with their families. // ⑪Sometimes / they laughed together, / and sometimes / they cried together. // ⑫Our lives today / are the same / as theirs were. // ⑬The movie shows / that such ordinary lives / are really precious. // (122 words)

🔊)) 意味のまとまりに注意して，本文全体を音読しよう！

New Words 新出単語の意味を調べよう			
gradually 副 [grǽdʒu(ə)li] A2	1.	niece 名 [níːs] B1	2.
raid 名 [réɪd]	3.	unexploded 形 [Ànɪksplóʊdɪd]	4.
explode 動 [ɪksplóʊd] B2	5.	ill 形 [íl] A2	6.

A Comprehension
パラグラフの要点を整理しよう

Fill in the blanks in Japanese. 【思考力・判断力・表現力】

戦況の悪化	すずと姪は (1. _____) にあう。
	→不発弾の爆発で，すずは (2. _____) を失い，姪は亡くなる。
終戦	終戦から4か月後：すずは愛する人たちを失ったことを知る。
	→「新型爆弾」によって両親が亡くなった。(3. _____) は病床に伏している。
映画を通してわかること	
・戦時中の人々も，今の私たちと同じように，ふつうの (4. _____) をしていた。	
・ふつうの生活がとても尊い。	

B Key Sentences
重要文について理解しよう

Fill in the blanks and translate the following sentences.
【知識・技能】【思考力・判断力・表現力】

① **Gradually, the situation gets worse.**

◆ worse は bad の比較級であり, 比較の対象は明示されていないが, 「これまでよりも」を補って解釈する。

訳： _____

⑤ **About four months after the war ends, <u>Suzu</u> <u>finds</u> "the new bomb" has**
　taken the lives of her mother and father.
　　　　　　　　　　　　S　　　V　　　　　　　O

◆ S + V + O (= that-節) の文。finds の後には that が省略されている。

訳： _____

_____

⑦ **She has lost |people| she loves.**

◆ she loves は people を修飾している。people の後には目的格の関係代名詞 1. _____ が省略
　されている。

訳： _____

⑧ **Through the movie, <u>we</u> <u>can find out</u> <u>how people lived during the war.</u>**
　　　　　　　　　　　　S　　　V　　　　　　O

◆【S + V + O (=疑問詞節)】how 以下の疑問詞節が文の目的語になっている。(→ **Grammar**)

訳： _____

⑫ **Our lives today are the same as theirs were.**

◆ theirs = their 2. _____ であり，つまり「戦時中の人々の生活」を指している。

訳： _____

🔊 意味のまとまりに注意して，本文全体を聞こう！

1 ①There are a lot of stores and restaurants / around us. // ②We take it for granted / that some of them are open / for 24 hours. // ③This business model has been popular. // ④It has brought us some advantages. //

2 ⑤First, / our lives have become convenient. // ⑥At a convenience store, / we can buy things, / pay bills, / and mail packages / at any time. // ⑦People / who work late at night / can eat / at a 24-hour restaurant / before or after work. //

3 ⑧Second, / our lives have become safer / thanks to 24-hour stores and restaurants. // ⑨People in danger / can ask for help / there. // ⑩Analysts tell us / that convenience stores play the role / of *koban*, / or police boxes, / especially at night. // (111 words)

🔊 意味のまとまりに注意して，本文全体を音読しよう！

New Words 新出単語の意味を調べよう			
grant 動 [grǽnt] B1	1.	advantage 名 [ədvǽntɪdʒ] A2	2.
bill 名 [bíl] A2	3.	analyst 名 [ǽn(ə)lɪst] B2	4.

A Comprehension
パラグラフの要点を整理しよう

Fill in the blanks in Japanese. 　　　　　【思考力・判断力・表現力】

24時間営業
・当たり前の存在になっており，ビジネスモデルとしても一般的になっている。
・いくつかのメリットがある。

> メリット①：生活が (1.　　　　　　　) になる
> ・買い物，請求書の支払い，小包の (2.　　　　　　) がいつでもできる。
> ・夜遅くに働く人が，仕事の前後に食事ができる。

> メリット②：生活がより (3.　　　　　　) になる
> ・危険な目にあったときに店に助けを求めることができる。
> ・夜はコンビニエンスストアが (4.　　　　　) の役割を果たす。

B Key Sentences
重要文について理解しよう

Fill in the blanks and translate the following sentences.
【知識・技能】【思考力・判断力・表現力】

② We take it for granted that some of them are open for 24 hours.

◆ take it for granted that ...で「…ということを当然だと思う」という意味。形式目的語itの具体的内容が that以下である。

◆ them＝1.＿＿＿＿＿＿＿＿＿＿＿＿＿＿＿＿＿＿＿＿＿＿＿

訳：＿＿＿＿＿＿＿＿＿＿＿＿＿＿＿＿＿＿＿＿＿＿＿＿＿＿＿＿＿＿

⑦ People who work late at night can eat at a 24-hour restaurant before or after work.

◆ 関係代名詞whoが導く関係詞節が先行詞peopleを修飾している。

◆ orは前置詞の2.＿＿＿＿＿＿＿と 3.＿＿＿＿＿＿＿ をつなぎ，その両方がworkにかかっている。

訳：＿＿＿＿＿＿＿＿＿＿＿＿＿＿＿＿＿＿＿＿＿＿＿＿＿＿＿＿＿

⑩ Analysts tell us that convenience stores play the role of *koban*, or police
　　　　　　 S　　 V　 O 　　　　　　　　　　　　　　　　　　O
boxes, especially at night.

◆ 【S＋V＋O＋O（＝that-節）】that以下全体が2つ目の目的語になっている。（→ Grammar）

◆ ここでのorは言いかえを表す用法で，「すなわち」の意味。*koban*をpolice boxesと言いかえている。

訳：＿＿＿＿＿＿＿＿＿＿＿＿＿＿＿＿＿＿＿＿＿＿＿＿＿＿＿＿＿

Lesson 7

Should Stores Stay Open for 24 Hours? Part 2

教科書 p.98-99

◀)) 意味のまとまりに注意して，本文全体を聞こう！

1 ①Convenience stores started / with an ice shop / in the U.S. / in the 1920s. //

②Later, / the ice shop started / to sell daily necessities and food / as well. // ③In the 1970s, / this idea came to Japan. // ④Unlike convenience stores now, / stores at that time / were only open / from early in the morning / till late at night. //

2 ⑤Until the 1970s, / there were almost no stores or restaurants / open at night / in Japan. // ⑥Many Japanese people / at that time / worked / during the day / and stayed home / at night. //

3 ⑦The Japanese economy developed rapidly, / especially in the early 1970s. // ⑧There was social demand / for people / to work / at night. // ⑨The change / in people's working styles / allowed around-the-clock stores / to appear / in Japan. // ⑩Now, / 24-hour convenience stores / can be seen everywhere. // (125 words)

◀)) 意味のまとまりに注意して，本文全体を音読しよう！

New Words 新出単語の意味を調べよう			
necessity 名 [nəsésəti] B2	1.	unlike 前 [ʌ̀nláɪk] B2	2.
economy 名 [ɪká(:)nəmi] B1	3.	rapidly 副 [rǽpɪdli] B1	4.
demand 名 [dɪmǽnd] B1	5.	allow 動 [əláʊ] A2	6.
around-the-clock 形 [əràʊndðəklá(:)k]	7.		

A Comprehension
パラグラフの要点を整理しよう

Fill in the blanks in Japanese.　　【思考力・判断力・表現力】

コンビニエンスストアの歴史	
1920年代	・アメリカの氷販売店が(1.　　　　　)や食料品を売り始め，コンビニエンスストアのルーツとなる。 ▼ ・日本では，多くの人が(2.　　　　　)に働き，夜は家にいた。 　→夜に営業している店や(3.　　　　　)はほとんどなかった。
1970年代	・急速な(4.　　　　　)により，日本でも夜間に働く人が増えた。 　→働き方の変化に合わせて，24時間営業店舗が登場。
現在	・24時間営業のコンビニエンスストアが一般的になった。

B Key Sentences
重要文について理解しよう

Fill in the blanks and translate the following sentences.
【知識・技能】【思考力・判断力・表現力】

④ Unlike convenience stores now, <u>stores at that time</u> <u>were</u> only <u>open</u> from
　S　　　　　　　　　　　　　　　　　V　　　　　C
early in the morning till late at night.

◆ unlikeは「…と違って」という意味で，品詞は(1.　　　　　)。

訳：_____

⑤ Until the 1970s, there were almost no <u>stores or restaurants</u> (open at
night) in Japan.

◆ There is構文である。「(～には)…がある」という意味。
◆ (almost no) stores or restaurantsを，形容詞openがat nightをともなって後ろから修飾している。

訳：_____

⑨ <u>The change in people's working styles</u> <u>allowed</u> <u>around-the-clock stores</u>
　S　　　　　　　　　　　　　　　　　　V　　　　　O
to appear in Japan.
to-不定詞

◆ S＋V＋O＋to-不定詞の文。allow ... to ～で「…が～できるようにする」という意味。

訳：_____

⑩ Now, 24-hour convenience stores can be seen everywhere.

◆【助動詞＋受け身】助動詞can＋be＋過去分詞で「～される(ことができる)」。(→Grammar)

訳：_____

Should Stores Stay Open for 24 Hours? Part 3

教科書 p.100-101

🔊 意味のまとまりに注意して，本文全体を聞こう！

1 ①It is true / that 24-hour stores have some advantages, / but they also have disadvantages. // ②For example, / they contribute to environmental problems. // ③Opening stores / for 24 hours / requires a lot of energy / and emits CO₂. // ④In addition, / stores throw away much unsold food. //

2 ⑤A labor shortage / is another problem. // ⑥Due to the falling birthrate / and aging population, / the number of people / who can work / late at night / has been decreasing. // ⑦Owners of convenience stores think / that it is difficult / to employ enough staff members. //

3 ⑧Should stores stay open / for 24 hours? // ⑨It is time / to think / about what our society really needs. // ⑩Some stores have stopped / opening for 24 hours. // ⑪Time will tell. // (112 words) 🔊 意味のまとまりに注意して，本文全体を音読しよう！

New Words 新出単語の意味を調べよう			
disadvantage 名 [dìsədvǽntɪdʒ] A2	1.	contribute 動 [kəntríbjət] B1	2.
require 動 [rɪkwáɪər] B1	3.	emit 動 [ɪmít]	4.
unsold 形 [ʌnsóʊld]	5.	labor 名 [léɪbər] A2	6.
shortage 名 [ʃɔ́ːrtɪdʒ] B1	7.	birthrate 名 [bə́ːrθrèɪt]	8.
population 名 [pὰ(ː)pjəléɪʃ(ə)n] A2	9.	decrease 動 [dìːkríːs] B1	10.
employ 動 [ɪmplɔ́ɪ] B2	11.		

A Comprehension
パラグラフの要点を整理しよう

Fill in the blanks in Japanese.　　【思考力・判断力・表現力】

24時間営業店舗のデメリット
① (1.　　　　　　)の原因になる。
・24時間営業するには多くのエネルギーが必要であり，二酸化炭素も排出する。
・売れ残った食品がたくさん(2.　　　　　　)されている。
② (3.　　　　　　)不足の問題がある。
・出生率の低下と高齢化により，深夜に働ける人材が減っていて，人員確保が難しい。

24時間営業は必要か？ → (4.　　　　　　)が本当に必要としているものについて考えるべき。
24時間営業をやめている店舗もある。

B Key Sentences
重要文について理解しよう

Fill in the blanks and translate the following sentences.
【知識・技能】【思考力・判断力・表現力】

① **It is true that 24-hour stores have some advantages, but they also have disadvantages.**

◆ It is true that ..., but 〜は「なるほど…だが，〜」という譲歩の意味を表す。

訳：_____

⑥ **Due to the falling birthrate and aging population, the number of people who can work late at night has been decreasing.**

◆ has been decreasingは現在完了進行形で，「(ずっと)減少している」という継続を表している。

◆ whoは主格の関係代名詞で，who can work late at nightの節全体が先行詞peopleを修飾している。

訳：_____

⑦ **Owners of convenience stores think that it is difficult to employ enough staff members.**

◆ that-節内は，形式主語のitを用いたit is ... to 〜（〜することは…だ）の構文になっている。

訳：_____

⑨ **It is time to think about what our society really needs.**

◆【関係代名詞what】whatは先行詞を含む関係代名詞で，「〜すること[もの]」という意味。この文では，what our society really needsが前置詞 1._____ の目的語になっている。（→ Grammar）

訳：_____

Should Stores Stay Open for 24 Hours? Part 4

教科書 p.102-103

🔊 意味のまとまりに注意して，本文全体を聞こう！

David: ① Do you think / stores should stay open / for 24 hours? //

Taro: ② Yes. // ③ They're essential / for us / in modern society. // ④ I wonder / how people had lived / before convenience stores started. // ⑤ Thanks to 24-hour stores, / we can buy things / at night. //

David: ⑥ I see. // ⑦ You mean / our lives have become convenient. // ⑧ How about you, / Kumi? //

Kumi: ⑨ I don't think / stores should stay open / for 24 hours. // ⑩ Going shopping / late at night / can be dangerous. // ⑪ There are a lot of crimes, / especially at night. // ⑫ I really think / we have to find new lifestyles / without 24-hour stores. //

David: ⑬ That's interesting. // ⑭ We have to change our way / of thinking, / right? // ⑮ In Europe, / most stores are closed / at night. // ⑯ I hear / that self-service stores will become more common / in Japan. // (120 words)

🔊 意味のまとまりに注意して，本文全体を音読しよう！

New Words 新出単語の意味を調べよう			
essential 形 [ɪsénʃ(ə)l] B1	1.	crime 名 [kráɪm] A2	2.
lifestyle 名 [láɪfstàɪl] A2	3.	self-service 形 [sèlfsə́ːrvəs] B1	4.
common 形 [kɑ́(ː)mən] A2	5.		

A Comprehension パラグラフの要点を整理しよう　Fill in the blanks in Japanese.　【思考力・判断力・表現力】

ディスカッション：店は24時間営業すべきか		
太郎の意見	Yes	・現代社会になくてはならない。 ・24時間営業店舗のおかげで(1.　　　　　)も買い物ができる。
久美の意見	No	・夜は(2.　　　　　)が多く，買い物に行くのは危険。 ・24時間営業店舗のない新しい生活様式を見つけるべき。
デイヴィッド先生の コメント		・私たちは(3.　　　　　)を変えないといけない。 ・ヨーロッパでは，多くの店は夜には閉まる。 ・日本では(4.　　　　　)の店がより広まっていくらしい。

B Key Sentences 重要文について理解しよう　Fill in the blanks and translate the following sentences.

【知識・技能】【思考力・判断力・表現力】

④ **I wonder how people had lived before convenience stores started.**

◆ I wonder ...は「…だろうか，…かしら」という意味。

◆【過去完了形】過去完了形had livedは過去のある時点までの状態の継続を表している。ここでは，convenience stores startedの時点まで「(ずっと)生活していた」という意味になる。(→ **Grammar**)

訳：

⑨ **I don't think stores should stay open for 24 hours.**

◆ thinkの後には 1.＿＿＿＿＿ が省略されている。

◆ that-節内はＳ＋Ｖ＋Ｃになっている。「Ｓ＝Ｃ」，つまり「店＝開いている」という関係。

訳：

⑩ <u>**Going shopping late at night**</u> <u>**can be**</u> <u>**dangerous.**</u>
　　　　　　　 S　　　　　　　　　　 V　　　 C

◆ 動名詞goingを含む句が主語になっており，Ｓ＋Ｖ＋Ｃの文になっている。

◆ 助動詞 2.＿＿＿＿＿ は可能性を表し，「～することもある，～しうる」という意味。

訳：

⑫ **I really think we have to find new lifestyles without 24-hour stores.**

◆ without 24-hour storesはnew lifestylesを後ろから修飾している。

訳：

Our Future with Artificial Intelligence **Part 1**

教科書 p.112-113

■)) 意味のまとまりに注意して，本文全体を聞こう！

1 ①AI has been an important issue / for us. // ②Some people talk / about the bright future / that AI will bring us. // ③Others worry / that AI may take away our jobs. // ④Let's look at the figures below, / and consider these differences / in attitudes / toward AI. //

2 ⑤Figure 1 shows / that 41.8% of people / in their twenties / worry about losing their jobs / due to AI. // ⑥On the other hand, / only 19.9% of people / aged over 60 / worry about it. // ⑦Younger people feel more uneasy / about this negative side / of AI. //

3 ⑧Concerning other areas / of AI, / Figure 2 shows / that younger people have more positive attitudes / toward AI. // ⑨About 10% of people / in their twenties and thirties / think / AI will have a favorable impact / on their lives. // ⑩About half this percentage / of older people / have positive images / of AI. // (134 words)

■)) 意味のまとまりに注意して，本文全体を音読しよう！

New Words 新出単語の意味を調べよう

gap 名 [gǽp] B1	1.	attitude 名 [ǽtətjùːd] A2	2.
issue 名 [íʃuː] A2	3.	consider 動 [kənsídər] A2	4.
uneasy 形 [ʌníːzi] A2	5.	negative 形 [négətɪv] A2	6.
concerning 前 [kənsə́ːrnɪŋ] B2	7.	favorable 形 [féɪv(ə)rəb(ə)l] B1	8.
impact 名 [ímpækt] A2	9.	percentage 名 [pərséntɪdʒ] B2	10.
image 名 [ímɪdʒ] A2	11.		

A Comprehension
パラグラフの要点を整理しよう

Fill in the blanks in Japanese.　　　　　　　【思考力・判断力・表現力】

AIに対して	肯定派	AIは明るい(1.　　　　　　　　)をもたらしてくれる。	
	否定派	AIが人間の(2.　　　　　　　　)を奪うかもしれない。	
グラフ1➡若い人たちのほうが，AIのせいで仕事を失うことに(3.　　　　　　　)を感じている。			
グラフ2➡若い人たちのほうが，AIが(4.　　　　　　　　)によい影響を与えてくれると考えている。			

B Key Sentences
重要文について理解しよう

Fill in the blanks and translate the following sentences.

【知識・技能】【思考力・判断力・表現力】

② **Some people talk about** ⌐the bright future¬ **that AI will bring us.　Others worry that AI may take away our jobs.**

◆【Some (people) ....　Others 〜.】「…する人もいれば，〜する人もいる」という意味で，some (people) とothersが対比的に述べられている。(→ **Grammar**)

◆ thatは目的格の関係代名詞で，that以下の節全体が先行詞the bright futureを修飾している。

訳：_____

_____

⑤ **Figure 1 shows that 41.8% of people in their twenties worry about losing their jobs due to AI.**

◆ 図やグラフなどの無生物主語に動詞showを用いて，「(図やグラフは)…を示している，(図やグラフによると)…だとわかる」という意味を表す。

訳：_____

⑧ **Concerning other areas of AI, Figure 2 shows that younger people have more positive attitudes toward AI.**

◆ concerningの品詞は(1.　　　　　　　　　)で，「…に関して，…について」の意味。

訳：_____

⑨ <u>**About 10% of people in their twenties and thirties**</u> <u>**think**</u> <u>**AI will have a**</u>
　　　　　　　　　　　　　S　　　　　　　　　　　　　　　V　　　O
<u>**favorable impact on their lives.**</u>

◆ S＋V＋O (＝that-節) の文。thinkの後にthatが省略されている。

◆ have a ... impact on 〜で「〜に…な影響を与える」という意味。

訳：_____

🔊 意味のまとまりに注意して，本文全体を聞こう！

1 ①We often talk about AI, / but what is it exactly? // ②It is a computer program / which can do a lot of tasks / with accuracy. // ③It repeats the tasks, / keeping its accuracy / over a long time. // ④Even human-level AI / can be realized / by deep learning. //

2 ⑤Deep learning is a technology / which enables a machine / to learn / by itself, / like humans do. // ⑥This type of AI / discovers different features / in an object / and repeats the process / until it can recognize the object. // ⑦As a result, / it can learn / to tell an object from others / with accuracy. //

3 ⑧This technology is used / for self-driving cars. // ⑨The AI recognizes stop signs / and traffic lights, / so the self-driving cars stop precisely / at intersections. // ⑩Traffic lane lines are recognized, / so cars keep / within their own lanes. // ⑪AI contributes to safe driving. // (134 words)

New Words 新出単語の意味を調べよう			
exactly 副 [ɪgzǽk(t)li] A2	1.	task 名 [tǽsk] A2	2.
accuracy 名 [ǽkjərəsi] B1	3.	human-level 形 [hjúːmənlèv(ə)l]	4.
enable 動 [ɪnéɪb(ə)l] B1	5.	feature 名 [fíːtʃər] A2	6.
object 名 [ɑ́(ː)bdʒekt] B1	7.	process 名 [prɑ́(ː)ses] B1	8.
recognize 動 [rékəgnàɪz] B1	9.	self-driving 形 [sèlfdráɪvɪŋ]	10.
precisely 副 [prɪsáɪsli] B2	11.	intersection 名 [ìntərsékʃ(ə)n] B2	12.
lane 名 [léɪn] A2	13.	within 前 [wɪðín] A2	14.

🔊 意味のまとまりに注意して，本文全体を音読しよう！

A Comprehension パラグラフの要点を整理しよう　Fill in the blanks in Japanese.　【思考力・判断力・表現力】

AIとは

…多くのタスクを正確にこなし続けることのできるコンピュータプログラム。

ディープラーニングによって（1.　　　　　　）レベルのAIも実現可能。

　　→ 人間のように（2.　　　　　　）が自分で学習できるようにする技術。自動運転車にも使われている。

自動運転車

・AIが停止標識や（3.　　　　　　）を認識し，（4.　　　　　　）で適切に止まることができる。

・車線を認識し，車線からはみ出さずに走行することができる。

B Key Sentences 重要文について理解しよう　Fill in the blanks and translate the following sentences.
【知識・技能】【思考力・判断力・表現力】

③ **It repeats the tasks, keeping its accuracy over a long time.**

◆ Itは前文のItと同じく 1.＿＿＿＿＿＿ を指している。

◆【分詞構文（付帯状況）】現在分詞のkeepingで始まる句が，「〜しながら」という付帯状況を表している。

（→ **Grammar**）

訳：＿＿＿＿＿＿＿＿＿＿＿＿＿＿＿＿＿＿＿

⑤ **Deep learning is a technology which enables a machine to learn by itself, like humans do.**
　　　　　　　　　　　　　　　代動詞

◆ whichは主格の関係代名詞で，which以下の節全体が先行詞a technologyを修飾している。

◆ このdoは代動詞といい，前に出た動詞の重複を避けるために用いられる。ここでは直前のlearnを指している。

訳：＿＿＿＿＿＿＿＿＿＿＿＿＿＿＿＿＿＿＿

⑧ **This technology is used for self-driving cars.**

◆ This technology = 2.＿＿＿＿＿＿＿

訳：＿＿＿＿＿＿＿＿＿＿＿＿＿＿＿＿＿＿＿

⑩ **Traffic lane lines are recognized, so cars keep within their own lanes.**

◆ 前半の節は動作主（by …）の示されていない受け身になっている。

訳：＿＿＿＿＿＿＿＿＿＿＿＿＿＿＿＿＿＿＿

Our Future with Artificial Intelligence Part 3

教科書 p.118-119

🔊 意味のまとまりに注意して，本文全体を聞こう！

1 ①AI is used / in facial recognition technology / at airports. // ②Passengers now often need / to wait / in lines / and show their passports and boarding passes / at gates. // ③Thanks to this technology, / however, / they won't need / to do these things, / and they can save travel time. //

2 ④AI is also useful / for predicting the times / when crimes are likely to happen. // ⑤It can predict the places / where crimes will happen, / too. // ⑥By using this technology, / police officers can prevent crimes / from happening. // ⑦As the number of crimes decreases, / society will become safer. //

3 ⑧AI, / however, / has some negative features. // ⑨For example, / it is becoming difficult / for even AI engineers / to understand AI's way / of thinking / exactly. // ⑩Considering the negative features, / we must try / to use AI carefully. //

(123 words) 🔊 意味のまとまりに注意して，本文全体を音読しよう！

New Words 新出単語の意味を調べよう

facial 形 [féɪʃ(ə)l]	1.	recognition 名 [rèkəgníʃ(ə)n] B2	2.
passenger 名 [pǽsɪn(d)ʒər] A2	3.	predict 動 [prɪdíkt] A2	4.
likely 形 [láɪkli] A2	5.	prevent 動 [prɪvént] A2	6.

A Comprehension
パラグラフの要点を整理しよう

Fill in the blanks in Japanese.　【思考力・判断力・表現力】

AIの 活用分野	①空港での（1.　　　　　　）システム 　列に並び，ゲートでパスポートと（2.　　　　　　　）を見せる必要がなくなる。 ➡時間短縮が可能に
	②犯罪予測 　犯罪が起きそうな（3.　　　　　）と場所を予測でき，犯罪を未然に防げる。 ➡犯罪の減少，（4.　　　　　）な社会の実現
AIのネガティブな側面 …開発者ですらAIがどのように考えるか理解するのが難しくなっている。	

B Key Sentences
重要文について理解しよう

Fill in the blanks and translate the following sentences.

【知識・技能】【思考力・判断力・表現力】

③ **Thanks to this technology, however, they won't need to do these things, and they can save travel time.**

◆ need to 〜は「〜する必要がある」という意味。won'tは 1.＿＿＿＿＿＿＿＿＿ notの短縮形。

◆ this technology = facial recognition technology, they = 2.＿＿＿＿＿＿

訳：

④ **AI is also useful for predicting the times when crimes are likely to happen.**

◆【関係副詞（when）】whenは「…する（とき）」を表す関係副詞で，when以下の節全体が先行詞the times を修飾している。（→ Grammar）

訳：

⑤ **It can predict the places where crimes will happen, too.**

◆【関係副詞（where）】whereは「…する（場所）」を表す関係副詞で，where以下の節全体が先行詞the places を修飾している。（→ Grammar）

訳：

⑨ **For example, it is becoming difficult for even AI engineers to understand AI's way of thinking exactly.**

◆ it is ... for A to 〜の構文で，動詞がis becomingなので，「Aが〜するのは…になってきている」という 意味。

訳：

🔊 意味のまとまりに注意して，本文全体を聞こう！

1 ①Local governments are trying / to use AI / to offer better medical services / to their citizens. // ②When a small child suddenly gets sick, / young parents often feel uneasy. // ③There is now an AI system / that can give helpful advice / to uneasy parents. // ④The way / they use the system / is by entering medical information / into their computers or smartphones. //

2 ⑤The AI system also helps / to relieve the burdens / of people / working in emergency medical services. // ⑥Emergency calls come / one after another, / especially after local clinics are closed. // ⑦The AI system can try / to cope with emergency cases / before workers do. //

3 ⑧AI will be used / in more fields, / and it will improve our quality / of life. // ⑨We will be able to live well / with AI / if we can make good use of it. // (130 words)

🔊 意味のまとまりに注意して，本文全体を音読しよう！

New Words 新出単語の意味を調べよう			
medical 形 [médɪk(ə)l] A2	1.	citizen 名 [sítəz(ə)n] A2	2.
relieve 動 [rɪlíːv] B2	3.	burden 名 [bə́ːrd(ə)n] B1	4.
emergency 形 [ɪmə́ːrdʒ(ə)nsi]	5.	clinic 名 [klínɪk] B1	6.
cope 動 [kóʊp] B2	7.	quality 名 [kwá(ː)ləti] A2	8.

A **Comprehension**
パラグラフの要点を整理しよう

Fill in the blanks in Japanese.　【思考力・判断力・表現力】

医療分野でのAI活用		
親	子供が急病になった際，コンピュータやスマートフォンで情報を入力　→	AI
	←　AIシステムが役立つ(1.　　　　)を提供してくれる	
➡救急での初期対応をAIが代替。救急医療の現場で働く人たちの(2.　　　　)を軽減。		

▼

・AIはより多くの分野で使われるようになり，生活の(3.　　　　)を向上させてくれる。
・有効に活用すればAIとうまく(4.　　　　)できる。

B **Key Sentences**
重要文について理解しよう

Fill in the blanks and translate the following sentences.
【知識・技能】【思考力・判断力・表現力】

③ There is now an AI system that can give helpful advice to uneasy parents.

◆ There is構文で，「…がある」という意味。

◆ thatは主格の関係代名詞で，that以下の節が先行詞an AI systemを修飾している。

訳：

④ The way they use the system is by entering medical information into their computers or smartphones.

◆【関係副詞】the way＋S＋Vで「SがVする方法」という意味（＝how＋S＋V）。(→ **Grammar**)

◆ このbyは「…によって」という手段や方法を表す用法。動名詞を続けてby ～ingとすると「～することによって」という意味になる。

訳：

⑥ Emergency calls come one after another, especially after local clinics are closed.
　　　　S　　　　　V

◆ S＋Vの文。このcallの品詞は(1.　　　　)である。

訳：

⑨ We will be able to live well with AI if we can make good use of it.

◆ 未来を表す助動詞willと可能を表すbe able to ～がいっしょに用いられている。

◆ it ＝ 2.＿＿＿＿＿

訳：

Stop Microplastic Pollution!

Part 1

教科書 p.128-129

🔊 意味のまとまりに注意して，本文全体を聞こう！

Manabu 2 hours ago //

①This afternoon, / I went to a café / with Takashi. // ②I ordered some iced coffee / as usual, / but something was different / today. // ③The person / at the counter / didn't give me a plastic straw. // ④She said, / "We have stopped / serving plastic straws / globally. // ⑤We want / to help / to save the environment / from microplastic pollution." //

⑥What are microplastics? // ⑦I searched for information / about the microplastic problem / on the Internet, / and I learned / that it is becoming very serious. // ⑧I was shocked. // ⑨The government / in every country / should make its people / stop wasting plastic products. //

⑩Now, / I really want / to do something / to solve this problem. // ⑪Let's discuss the problem together. //

Takashi 30 minutes ago //

⑫We use a lot of plastics / every day. // ⑬Should we stop using them? //

Vivian 45 minutes ago //

⑭What can we do / about this? //

Kumi 1 hour ago //

⑮I had no idea / about this problem. // (149 words)

🔊 意味のまとまりに注意して，本文全体を音読しよう！

New Words 新出単語の意味を調べよう			
iced 形 [áɪst]	1.	counter 名 [káʊntər] B2	2.
straw 名 [strɔ́ː] B1	3.	globally 副 [glóʊb(ə)li] B2	4.
microplastic 名 [màɪkrouplǽstɪk]	5.		

A Comprehension
パラグラフの要点を整理しよう

Fill in the blanks in Japanese.

【思考力・判断力・表現力】

学の投稿
カフェでアイスコーヒーを注文したら，プラスチック製の(1.　　　　　　)が付いていなかった。 マイクロプラスチック汚染から(2.　　　　　)を守るため。 　…マイクロプラスチック汚染は非常に(3.　　　　　)な問題になっている。各国の政府が国民 　にプラスチック製品の(4.　　　　　)をやめさせるべきだ。この問題を解決するために何か 　したい。

B Key Sentences
重要文について理解しよう

Fill in the blanks and translate the following sentences.

【知識・技能】【思考力・判断力・表現力】

③ The person at the counter didn't give me a plastic straw.
　　　　　S　　　　　　　　V　　O₁　　O₂

◆ S＋V＋O₁＋O₂の文。前置詞句at the counterがthe personを後ろから修飾して，全体が主語になっている。

訳：_____

④ She said, "We have stopped serving plastic straws globally. We want to help to save the environment from microplastic pollution."

◆ have stoppedは完了・結果を表す現在完了形。動名詞servingがhave stoppedの(1.　　　　　)になっている。

◆ want to ～は「～したい」，help to ～は「～するのに役立つ，～する手助けをする」という意味。

訳：_____
　　_____

⑨ The government in every country should make its people stop wasting
　　　　　　　　　　　S　　　　　　　　V　　　　O　　　C
plastic products.

◆【S＋V＋O＋C (＝原形不定詞)】使役動詞make＋O＋C (＝原形不定詞)で「Oに～させる」という意味になる。(→ **Grammar**)

訳：_____

⑩ Now, I really want to do something to solve this problem.

◆ to solveは不定詞の副詞用法で，「～するために」という目的を表す。to以下が動詞doを修飾している。

◆ this problem ＝ 2._____

訳：_____

Stop Microplastic Pollution!

Part 2

教科書 p.130-131

🔊 意味のまとまりに注意して，本文全体を聞こう！

1 ①When you walk / along the beach, / you may see a lot of small objects / shining in the sand. // ②Perhaps / they are "microplastics." //

2 ③"Micro" means "very small." // ④Microplastics are very small pieces / of plastic garbage. // ⑤They are less than about five millimeters / in diameter. // ⑥Plastics easily break / into small pieces / when they are heated / or exposed / to sunlight / for a long time. //

3 ⑦Wood pieces and grass / on the beach / can be eaten / by microbes, / but plastics often remain there. // ⑧Plastics may become smaller, / but they do not disappear / easily. // ⑨Most of them / may be washed down / into the sea / and stay there forever. // ⑩As a result, / the sea becomes the "dead end" / of the plastics / people throw away. // (117 words)

🔊 意味のまとまりに注意して，本文全体を音読しよう！

New Words 新出単語の意味を調べよう

sand 名 [sǽnd] B1	1.		micro 形 [máɪkrou]	2.	
millimeter 名 [míləmìːtər] B2	3.		diameter 名 [daɪǽmətər] B1	4.	
expose 動 [ɪkspóuz] B1	5.		sunlight 名 [sʌ́nlàɪt] A2	6.	
microbe 名 [máɪkroub] B2	7.		remain 動 [rɪméɪn] A2	8.	

A Comprehension パラグラフの要点を整理しよう　Fill in the blanks in Japanese.　　　　【思考力・判断力・表現力】

マイクロプラスチックとは
・プラスチックごみの非常に小さなかけらで，直径約(1.　　　　　　)以下。 ・プラスチックは，熱や(2.　　　　　　)に長時間さらされると細かく砕けやすくなる。 ・(3.　　　　　　)に分解される木や草と異なり，プラスチックは簡単にはなくならない。 　→プラスチックごみは(4.　　　　　　)に流され，ずっととどまり続ける。

B Key Sentences 重要文について理解しよう　Fill in the blanks and translate the following sentences.

【知識・技能】【思考力・判断力・表現力】

① When you walk along the beach, you may see a lot of small objects shining
　　　　　　　　　　　　　　　　　　 S　　 V　　　　　 O　　　　　　　　 C
in the sand.

◆【S＋V＋O＋C（＝現在分詞）】知覚動詞see＋O＋C（＝現在分詞）で「Oが〜しているのを見る」という
　意味になる。O＋Cは，A lot of small objects are shining. という関係になっている。(→**Grammar**)

訳：

⑥ Plastics easily break into small pieces when they are heated or exposed
to sunlight for a long time.

◆ they = 1.

◆ 後半のwhen-節の中は受け身になっている。are heatedと (are) exposed to sunlightが接続詞orによっ
　て並列に結ばれている。

訳：

⑨ Most of them may be washed down into the sea and stay there forever.
　　 S　　　　　 V₁　　　　　　　　　　　　　　　　　 V₂

◆ may be washed downは助動詞＋受け身のかたち。

◆ 2つの動詞may be washedと(may) stayが接続詞andによって並列に結ばれている。

訳：

⑩ As a result, the sea becomes the "dead end" of the plastics people throw
away.

◆ people throw awayはthe plasticsを修飾している。the plasticsの後には目的格の関係代名詞
　2.　　　　　　　 が省略されている。

訳：

Stop Microplastic Pollution! Part 3

教科書 p.132-133

◀) 意味のまとまりに注意して，本文全体を聞こう！

1 ①Microplastics are found / in the oceans / all over the world. // ②According to a study, / 2.4 pieces / of microplastics / were found / in every ton / of seawater, / even at several kilometers / away from the coast. // ③Now, / such polluted seawater / is called "plastic soup." //

2 ④Microplastics spread / through the food chain. // ⑤Plankton are near the bottom / of the food chain. // ⑥The plankton may eat microplastics / if they mistake them for their food. // ⑦Microplastic pollution spreads / as small fish eat plankton / and the bigger sea animals, / such as sharks and whales, / eat those small fish. //

3 ⑧Such a situation may be bad / for people's health / because people may eat fish / that have eaten microplastics. // ⑨In fact, / plastics are found / within the fishes' bodies. // (117 words)

◀) 意味のまとまりに注意して，本文全体を音読しよう！

New Words 新出単語の意味を調べよう			
according 副 [əkɔ́:rdɪŋ]	1. (according to ...)	ton 名 [tʌ́n] B2	2.
seawater 名 [síːwɔ̀ːtər] B1	3.	coast 名 [kóʊst] A2	4.
pollute 動 [pəlúːt] A2	5.	chain 名 [tʃéɪn] A2	6.
plankton 名 [plǽŋ(k)tən]	7.	shark 名 [ʃάːrk]	8.
whale 名 [(h)wéɪl] B1	9.		

A Comprehension
パラグラフの要点を整理しよう

Fill in the blanks in Japanese.

【思考力・判断力・表現力】

> マイクロプラスチック汚染の広がり方

▶マイクロプラスチックは世界中の海の中に見られ，（1.　　　　　　　）を通して広がる。

| プランクトンが，（2.　　　　　）と間違えてマイクロプラスチックを食べる。 | → | 小魚がそのプランクトンを食べる。 |

| より大きな（3.　　　　　）がその小魚を食べる。 | ← | 最終的に，マイクロプラスチックを取り込んだ魚を（4.　　　　　）が食べることになるかもしれない。 |

B Key Sentences
重要文について理解しよう

Fill in the blanks and translate the following sentences.

【知識・技能】【思考力・判断力・表現力】

① **Microplastics are found in the oceans all over the world.**

◆ We find microplastics in the oceans all over the world. を受け身にした文である。

訳：＿＿＿＿＿＿＿＿＿＿＿＿＿＿＿＿＿＿＿＿＿＿＿＿＿＿

③ **Now, such polluted seawater is called "plastic soup."**

◆ call＋A＋B「AをBと呼ぶ」の受け身である。A is called Bで「AはBと呼ばれる」の意味。

◆ such polluted seawaterとは，（1.　　　　　　　　　　　）に汚染された海水のこと。

◆ 過去分詞pollutedは 2.＿＿＿＿＿＿＿ を修飾している。

訳：＿＿＿＿＿＿＿＿＿＿＿＿＿＿＿＿＿＿＿＿＿＿＿＿＿＿

⑥ **The plankton may eat microplastics / if they mistake them for their food.**

◆【条件を表すif-節】if-節は条件を表す副詞節であり，「もし…なら」という意味。(→ **Grammar**)

◆ theyとtheirはプランクトンを，themはマイクロプラスチックを指している。

訳：＿＿＿＿＿＿＿＿＿＿＿＿＿＿＿＿＿＿＿＿＿＿＿＿＿＿

⑧ **Such a situation may be bad for people's health / because people may eat fish that have eaten microplastics.**

◆ because-節は理由を表す副詞節であり，「…なので」という意味。

◆ thatは主格の関係代名詞で，that以下の節が先行詞fishを修飾している。

訳：＿＿＿＿＿＿＿＿＿＿＿＿＿＿＿＿＿＿＿＿＿＿＿＿＿＿

Stop Microplastic Pollution!

Part 4

教科書 p.136-137

◀)) 意味のまとまりに注意して，本文全体を聞こう！

1 ①More and more countries / have taken action / to solve the microplastic problem. // ②They have tried / to cut the amount / of plastic / people use. // ③They hope / that fewer plastic products will be used / around the world. //

2 ④Even young people can help / to solve the problem. // ⑤For example, / an American girl made a submarine robot / to find microplastics / in the seawater. // ⑥Such robots may help / to clean the sea / in the future. //

3 ⑦Everybody can help / to change the situation. // ⑧You may say to yourself, / "Maybe / if I had a good idea, / I could do something useful." // ⑨However, / even if you don't have a very good idea, / you can say "no" / to some plastic products / and make the problem less serious. // ⑩Let's act / for a brighter future. // (124 words)

◀)) 意味のまとまりに注意して，本文全体を音読しよう！

New Words 新出単語の意味を調べよう

submarine 形 [sʌ́bməriːn]　1.

A Comprehension
パラグラフの要点を整理しよう

Fill in the blanks in Japanese.

【思考力・判断力・表現力】

マイクロプラスチック問題に対する取り組み
・各国で，使用するプラスチックの(1.　　　　　　)を削減しようとする動きがある。
・アメリカの女の子は，海中でマイクロプラスチックを見つける水中(2.　　　　　)を制作した。
・たとえいい解決策が浮かばなくても，(3.　　　　　)製品に「ノー」と言うことはできる。
➡だれもが状況を変える手助けをすることができる。より明るい(4.　　　　　)のために行動しよう。

B Key Sentences
重要文について理解しよう

Fill in the blanks and translate the following sentences.

【知識・技能】【思考力・判断力・表現力】

① More and more countries have taken action to solve the microplastic problem.

◆ to solve は目的を表す不定詞の副詞用法で，動詞 have taken を修飾している。

訳：＿＿＿＿＿＿＿＿＿＿＿＿＿＿＿＿＿＿＿＿＿＿＿＿＿＿＿＿＿

② They have tried to cut the amount of plastic people use.

◆ They = 1.＿＿＿＿＿＿＿＿＿＿＿＿＿＿＿＿

◆ people use は plastic を修飾している。plastic の後には目的格の関係代名詞 2.＿＿＿＿＿＿＿＿ が省略されている。

訳：＿＿＿＿＿＿＿＿＿＿＿＿＿＿＿＿＿＿＿＿＿＿＿＿＿＿＿＿＿

⑧ You may say to yourself, "Maybe if I had a good idea, I could do something useful."

◆【仮定法過去】〈If ＋ S ＋過去形 ..., S ＋ could ＋動詞の原形 〜〉で，「もし…ならば，〜できるのだが」という現在の事実に反する仮定を表す。(→ Grammar)

訳：＿＿＿＿＿＿＿＿＿＿＿＿＿＿＿＿＿＿＿＿＿＿＿＿＿＿＿＿＿

⑨ However, even if you don't have a very good idea, you can say "no" to some
plastic products and make the problem less serious.
S V1 O
V2 O C

◆ 主節の前半は S ＋ V ＋ O，後半は S ＋ V ＋ O ＋ C になっている。make ＋ O ＋ C で「O を C にする」の意味。

◆ can say と (can) make が接続詞 and によって並列に結ばれている。

訳：＿＿＿＿＿＿＿＿＿＿＿＿＿＿＿＿＿＿＿＿＿＿＿＿＿＿＿＿＿

＿＿＿＿＿＿＿＿＿＿＿＿＿＿＿＿＿＿＿＿＿＿＿＿＿＿＿＿＿＿＿

A Retrieved Reformation

Part 1

教科書 p.144-145

🔊 意味のまとまりに注意して，本文全体を聞こう！

1 ①Jimmy Valentine was released / from prison, / and it was just a week later / that a safe was broken open / in Richmond, / Indiana. // ②Eight hundred dollars was stolen. // ③Two weeks after that, / a safe / in Logansport / was opened, / and fifteen hundred dollars / was taken. // ④Everyone was shocked, / as this safe was so strong / that people thought / no one could break it open. // ⑤Then / a safe / in Jefferson City / was opened, / and five thousand dollars / was stolen. //

2 ⑥Ben Price was a detective. // ⑦He was a big man, / and famous for his skill / at solving very difficult and important cases. // ⑧So now / he began / to work / on these three cases. // ⑨He was the only person / who knew / how Jimmy did his job. // ⑩People / with safes / full of money / were glad / to hear / that Ben Price was at work / trying to arrest Mr. Valentine. //

3 ⑪One afternoon, / Jimmy Valentine and his suitcase / arrived in a small town / named Elmore. // ⑫Jimmy, / looking like an athletic young man / just home from college, / walked down the street / toward the hotel. //

4 ⑬A young lady walked / across the street, / passed him / at the corner, / and went through a door / with a sign / "The Elmore Bank" / on it. // ⑭Jimmy Valentine looked into her eyes, / forgot at once / what he was, / and became another man. // ⑮The young lady looked back at him, / and then lowered her eyes / as her face became red. // ⑯Handsome young men / like Jimmy / were not often seen / in Elmore. //

(241 words) 🔊 意味のまとまりに注意して，本文全体を音読しよう！

New Words 新出単語の意味を調べよう			
Jimmy Valentine [dʒími vǽləntàin]	ジミー・バレンタイン	release 動 [rɪlíːs] B1	1.
prison 名 [príz(ə)n] B1	2.	Richmond [rítʃmənd]	リッチモンド
Indiana [ìndiǽnə]	インディアナ州	stolen 動 [stóʊlən]	3. の過去分詞形
steal 動 [stíːl] A2	4.	Logansport [lóʊgənzpɔ̀ːrt]	ローガンズポート

Jefferson City [dʒéfərs(ə)nsíti]	ジェファーソンシティー	Ben Price [bén práɪs]	ベン・プライス
detective 名 [dɪtéktɪv] B1	5.	arrest 動 [ərést] B1	6
Elmore [élmɔːr]	エルモア	athletic 形 [æθlétɪk] B1	7.
lower 動 [lóuər] B2	8.		

A Comprehension
パラグラフの要点を整理しよう　Fill in the blanks in Japanese.　【思考力・判断力・表現力】

ジミー・バレンタインと若い女性の出会い	
ジミー・バレンタイン	・(1. 　　　　　)を出てから，リッチモンド，ローガンズポート，ジェファーソンシティーで(2. 　　　　　)をくり返す。 ・(3. 　　　　　)に到着後，エルモア銀行に入っていく若い女性に関心をもつ。
ベン・プライス	・有能な(4. 　　　　　)であり，金庫破りの事件でジミーを追っている。

B Key Sentences
重要文について理解しよう　Fill in the blanks and translate the following sentences.
【知識・技能】【思考力・判断力・表現力】

⑨ He was the only person who knew how Jimmy did his job.
　　S　V　　　　　C

◆ S＋V＋Cの文。Cにあたるthe only personは，主格の関係代名詞whoの先行詞になっている。

◆ how以下がknewの目的語で，間接疑問文になっている。

訳：＿＿＿＿＿＿＿＿＿＿＿＿＿＿＿＿＿＿＿＿＿＿＿＿＿＿＿＿＿＿＿＿＿＿＿＿

⑩ People with safes full of money were glad to hear that Ben Price was at
　　　　　　　S　　　　　　　　　　V　　C

work trying to arrest Mr. Valentine.

◆ withは所有を表す前置詞で，「…を持っている」の意味。形容詞句full of moneyが 1.＿＿＿＿＿＿＿
を後ろから修飾している。

◆ to hearは感情の原因を表す副詞用法の不定詞。be glad to hear ...で「…を聞いてうれしい」の意味。

訳：＿＿＿＿＿＿＿＿＿＿＿＿＿＿＿＿＿＿＿＿＿＿＿＿＿＿＿＿＿＿＿＿＿＿＿＿

　　　S　　　　　分詞構文　　　　　　　　　　　　　　　　　　　　　　V
⑫ Jimmy, / looking like an athletic young man just home from college, / walked

down the street toward the hotel.

◆ 文中に挿入された分詞構文looking ...はジミーの様子を描いている。

訳：＿＿＿＿＿＿＿＿＿＿＿＿＿＿＿＿＿＿＿＿＿＿＿＿＿＿＿＿＿＿＿＿＿＿＿＿

A Retrieved Reformation

Part 2

教科書 p.146-147

🔊 意味のまとまりに注意して，本文全体を聞こう！

1 ①Jimmy saw a boy / playing on the steps / of the bank / and began asking him questions / about the town. // ②After a time, / the young lady came out of the bank. // ③This time / she pretended / not to notice the young man / with the suitcase, / and went her way. // ④"Isn't that young lady Polly Simpson?" / Jimmy asked the boy. //

2 ⑤"No," / answered the boy. // ⑥"She's Annabel Adams. // ⑦Her father is the owner / of this bank." //

3 ⑧Jimmy went to the hotel. // ⑨He told the hotel clerk / that his name was Ralph D. Spencer, / and that he had come / to Elmore / to look for a place / where he could set up a shoe shop. // ⑩The clerk was so impressed / by Jimmy's clothes and manner / that he kindly gave him as much information / about the town / as he could. // ⑪Yes, / Elmore needed a good shoe shop. // ⑫It was a pleasant town / to live in, / and the people were friendly. //

4 ⑬"Mr. Spencer" told the hotel clerk / that he would like to stay / in the town / for a few days / and look over the situation. // ⑭Mr. Ralph D. Spencer, / Jimmy Valentine's new identity / —— an identity / created by a sudden attack of love / —— remained in Elmore / and opened a shoe shop. //

5 ⑮Soon / his shoe shop was doing a good business, / and he won the respect / of the community. // ⑯And more importantly, / he got to know Annabel Adams. // ⑰They fell deeply in love / and started / to plan their wedding. // (239 words)

🔊 意味のまとまりに注意して，本文全体を音読しよう！

New Words 新出単語の意味を調べよう

pretend 動 [priténd] A2	1.	Polly Simpson [pá(:)li sím(p)s(ə)n]	ポリー・シンプソン	
Annabel Adams [ǽnəbel ǽdəmz]	アナベル・アダムズ	Ralph D. Spencer [rǽlf díː spénsər]	ラルフ・D・スペンサー	
manner 名 [mǽnər] A2	2.	pleasant 形 [pléz(ə)nt] A2	3.	
identity 名 [aɪdéntəti] B1	4.	attack 名 [ətǽk] A2	5.	

community 名 [kəmjúːnəti] B2	6.	wedding 名 [wédɪŋ] A2	7.

A Comprehension
パラグラフの要点を整理しよう

Fill in the blanks in Japanese.　　　　　【思考力・判断力・表現力】

ジミー・バレンタインのエルモアでの暮らし		
ジミー・バレンタイン		・若い女性はアナベル・アダムズという名前だと知る。 ・ラルフ・D・スペンサーと名乗り，エルモアのホテルに滞在。ホテルの 　フロント係からこの町の(1.　　　　　)を聞き出す。 ・エルモアで(2.　　　　　)を開き，繁盛店となる。地域の人からも受 　け入れられる。
アナベル・アダムズ		・エルモア銀行のオーナーの(3.　　　　　)である。
➡ジミーとアナベルは知り合う。愛し合うようになり，(4.　　　　　)の準備を始める。		

B Key Sentences
重要文について理解しよう

Fill in the blanks and translate the following sentences.
【知識・技能】【思考力・判断力・表現力】

① <u>Jimmy</u> <u>saw</u> <u>a boy</u> <u>playing</u> on the steps of the bank and <u>began</u> <u>asking</u> him
　　S　　V₁　　O　　C　　　　　　　　　　　　　　　　　V₂　　O

questions about the town.

◆ 前半はS＋V＋O＋C（＝現在分詞）になっている。see＋O＋〜ingで「Oが〜しているのを見る」の意味。

◆ 後半は(S＋)V＋O（＝動名詞）になっている。begin 〜ingは「〜し始める」の意味。

訳：

⑩ The clerk was <u>so</u> impressed by Jimmy's clothes and manner <u>that</u> he

kindly gave him as much information about the town as he could.

◆ be impressed by ...という受け身の文の中にso ... that 〜「とても…なので〜」の表現が組み込まれている。

◆ he = 1.＿＿＿＿＿＿＿＿＿＿ , him = 2.＿＿＿＿＿＿

訳：

⑭ <u>Mr. Ralph D. Spencer</u>, Jimmy Valentine's new identity ── an identity created

by a sudden attack of love ── <u>remained</u> in Elmore and <u>opened</u> a shoe shop.
　　　　　　　　　　　　　　　　　　　　　　V₁　　　　　　　　　　V₂

◆ Mr. Ralph D. SpencerとJimmy Valentine's new identityは同格の関係であり，その後のダッシュに
　はさまれた部分がさらにどのようなidentityか言いかえている。

訳：

A Retrieved Reformation

Part 3

教科書 p.148-149

🔊 意味のまとまりに注意して，本文全体を聞こう！

1 ①One day, / Jimmy wrote a letter / to one of his old friends / in Little Rock. // ②The letter said, / "I want / to give you my tools. // ③You couldn't buy them / even for a thousand dollars. // ④I don't need them anymore / because I finished with the old business / a year ago. // ⑤I will never touch another man's money / again." //

2 ⑥It was a few days / after Jimmy sent his letter / that Ben Price secretly arrived / in Elmore. // ⑦He went around the town / in his quiet way / until he found out all / he wanted to know. // ⑧From a drugstore / across the street / from Spencer's shoe shop, / he watched Ralph D. Spencer / walk by. // ⑨"You think / you're going to marry the banker's daughter, / don't you, / Jimmy?" / said Ben / to himself, / softly. // ⑩"Well, / I'm not so sure / about that!" //

3 ⑪The next morning, / Jimmy had breakfast / at the Adams home. // ⑫That day, / he was going to Little Rock / to order his wedding suit, / buy something nice / for Annabel, / and give his tools away / to his friend. //

4 ⑬After breakfast, / several members / of the Adams family / went to the bank together / ——Mr. Adams, / Annabel, / Jimmy, / and Annabel's married sister / with her two little girls, / aged five and nine. // ⑭On the way to the bank, / they waited / outside Jimmy's shop / while he ran up to his room / and got his suitcase. // ⑮Then / they went on / to the bank. // (228 words)

🔊 意味のまとまりに注意して，本文全体を音読しよう！

New Words 新出単語の意味を調べよう			
Little Rock [lít(ə)lrà(:)k]	リトルロック	secretly 副 [síːkrətli] B1	1.
banker 名 [bǽŋkər] B2	2.	suit 名 [súːt] A2	3.

A Comprehension パラグラフの要点を整理しよう Fill in the blanks in Japanese. 【思考力・判断力・表現力】

ジミー・バレンタインの行動と心境の変化
・ジミーは友人に，金庫破りの (1.　　　　　) を譲るという手紙を書いた。 ・ベン・プライスがジミーを追ってエルモアに到着。 ・ジミーはアダムズ家での朝食後，アダムズ一家の数人とともに (2.　　　　　) に行った。 　　　　　　　→ 父，アナベル，(3.　　　　　) とその 2 人の娘 ・途中，(4.　　　　　) を取りにジミーの靴屋に寄った。

B Key Sentences 重要文について理解しよう Fill in the blanks and translate the following sentences.
【知識・技能】【思考力・判断力・表現力】

③ **You couldn't buy them even for a thousand dollars.**

◆ couldは低い可能性を表し，否定形のcouldn'tは可能性がまったくないことを表す。

◆ them = 1.＿＿＿＿＿＿＿＿＿＿＿＿＿＿＿

訳：＿＿＿＿＿＿＿＿＿＿＿＿＿＿＿＿＿＿＿＿＿＿＿＿＿＿＿

⑥ **It was a few days after Jimmy sent his letter that Ben Price secretly arrived in Elmore.**

◆ It was ... that 〜は強調構文で，「〜なのは…だった」という意味を表す。この文では，時を表す副詞句が強調されている。

訳：＿＿＿＿＿＿＿＿＿＿＿＿＿＿＿＿＿＿＿＿＿＿＿＿＿＿＿

⑧ **From a drugstore across the street from Spencer's shoe shop, he watched**
 S V
Ralph D. Spencer walk by.
 O C

◆ S＋V＋O＋C (＝原形不定詞)の文。watch＋O＋Cで「Oが〜するのを見る」の意味。

訳：＿＿＿＿＿＿＿＿＿＿＿＿＿＿＿＿＿＿＿＿＿＿＿＿＿＿＿

＿＿＿＿＿＿＿＿＿＿＿＿＿＿＿＿＿＿＿＿＿＿＿＿＿＿＿＿＿

⑭ **On the way to the bank, they waited outside Jimmy's shop while he ran up to his room and got his suitcase.**

◆ on the way to ...は「…の途中で」という意味。

◆ ここでのoutsideは前置詞で，「…の外で[に]」という意味。

訳：＿＿＿＿＿＿＿＿＿＿＿＿＿＿＿＿＿＿＿＿＿＿＿＿＿＿＿

＿＿＿＿＿＿＿＿＿＿＿＿＿＿＿＿＿＿＿＿＿＿＿＿＿＿＿＿＿

A Retrieved Reformation

Part 4

教科書 p.150-151

◀» 意味のまとまりに注意して，本文全体を聞こう！

1 ①They all went into the banking-room / —— Jimmy, / too, / for Mr. Adams' future son-in-law / was welcome / anywhere. // ②Everyone in the bank / was glad / to see the good-looking, nice young man / who was going to marry Annabel. // ③Jimmy put down the suitcase / in the corner / of the room. //

2 ④The Elmore Bank had just put in a new safe. // ⑤It was as large as a small room / and it had a very special new kind of door / that was controlled / by a clock. // ⑥Mr. Adams was very proud of this new safe / and was showing / how to set the time / when the door should open. // ⑦The two children, / May and Agatha, / enjoyed touching all the interesting parts / of its shining heavy door. //

3 ⑧While these things were happening, / Ben Price quietly entered the bank / and looked inside the banking-room. // ⑨He told the bank teller / that he didn't want anything; / he was just waiting / for a man / he knew. //

4 ⑩Suddenly, / there were screams / from the women. // ⑪May, / the five-year-old girl, / had firmly closed the door / of the safe / by accident, / and Agatha was inside! // ⑫Mr. Adams tried hard / to pull open the door / for a moment, / and then cried, / "The door can't be opened! // ⑬And the clock / —— I haven't started it / yet." //

5 ⑭"Please break it open!" / Agatha's mother cried out. //

6 ⑮"Quiet!" / said Mr. Adams, / raising a shaking hand. // ⑯"Everyone, / be quiet / for a moment. // ⑰Agatha!" / he called as loudly / as he could. // ⑱"Can you hear me?" // ⑲They could hear, / although not clearly, / the sound / of the child's voice. // ⑳In the darkness / inside the safe, / she was screaming / with fear. // ㉑Agatha's mother, / now getting more desperate, / started hitting the door / with her hands. // (277 words)

◀» 意味のまとまりに注意して，本文全体を音読しよう！

New Words 新出単語の意味を調べよう

banking-room 名 [bǽŋkɪŋrùːm]	1.	son-in-law 名 [sʌ́nɪnlɔ̀ː] B2	2.

good-looking 形 [gùdlúkɪŋ] A2	3.	control 動 [kəntróul] B1	4.
Agatha [ǽgəθə]	アガサ	teller 名 [télər] B1	5.
scream 名 動 [skríːm] A2・B1	6. 名 動	firmly 副 [fə́ːrmli] B1	7.
although 接 [ɔːlðóu] A2	8.	darkness 名 [dáːrknəs] B1	9.
fear 名 [fíər] A2	10.	desperate 形 [désp(ə)rət] B1	11.

A Comprehension パラグラフの要点を整理しよう　Fill in the blanks in Japanese.　【思考力・判断力・表現力】

銀行の執務室での出来事	
ジミー・バレンタイン	・(1.　　　　　　)を執務室の隅のほうに置く。
アダムズ氏	・(2.　　　　　　)で制御される最新型の金庫を紹介する。
ベン・プライス	・銀行に入り，(3.　　　　　　)内の様子を伺う。
アナベルの姉の娘	・メイが誤って金庫の扉を閉めてしまい，(4.　　　　　　)が金庫の中に閉じ込められてしまう。

B Key Sentences 重要文について理解しよう　Fill in the blanks and translate the following sentences.
【知識・技能】【思考力・判断力・表現力】

⑥ Mr. Adams was very proud of this new safe and was showing how to set the time when the door should open.

◆ whenは「…する(とき)」を表す関係副詞で，when以下の節が先行詞the timeを修飾している。

訳：

⑲ They could hear, / although not clearly, / the sound of the child's voice.
S　V　O

◆ although not clearlyという副詞節が文中に挿入されている。省略を補うと，although they could not 1.　　　　　 clearlyとなる。

訳：

分詞構文
㉑ Agatha's mother, / now getting more desperate, / started hitting the door with her hands.

◆ 文中に挿入されている(now) getting ...は分詞構文で，アガサの母親の状態を表している。

訳：

A Retrieved Reformation

Part 5

教科書 p.152-153

🔊 意味のまとまりに注意して，本文全体を聞こう！

1 ①Annabel turned to Jimmy. // ②Her large eyes were full of pain, / but not yet despairing. // ③A woman believes / that the man / she loves / can find a way / to do anything. // ④"Can't you do something, / Ralph? // ⑤Try, / won't you?" // ⑥He looked at her / with a strange, soft smile / on his lips / and in his eyes. //

2 ⑦"Annabel," / he said, / "give me that rose / you are wearing, / will you?" //

3 ⑧She couldn't understand / what he meant, / but she put the rose / in his hand. // ⑨Jimmy took it / and placed it / in the pocket / of his vest. // ⑩Then / he threw off his coat. // ⑪With that act, / Ralph D. Spencer disappeared, / and Jimmy Valentine took his place. // ⑫"Stay away from the door, / all of you," / he ordered. //

4 ⑬He placed his suitcase / on the table / and opened it. // ⑭From that time on, / he didn't pay any attention / to anyone else there. // ⑮Quickly / he laid the strange shining tools / on the table. // ⑯Nobody moved / as they watched him work. // ⑰Soon / Jimmy's drill was biting smoothly / into the steel door. // ⑱In ten minutes / —— faster / than he had ever done it before / —— he opened the door. //

5 ⑲Agatha, / completely exhausted / but unharmed, / ran into her mother's arms. // ⑳Jimmy Valentine silently put his coat back on / and walked / toward the front door / of the bank. // ㉑As he went, / he thought / he heard a voice call, / "Ralph!" // ㉒But he never hesitated. // ㉓At the door, / a big man was standing / in his way. // ㉔"Hello, Ben!" / said Jimmy. // ㉕"You're here / at last, / aren't you? // ㉖Well, / let's go. // ㉗I don't care now." //

6 ㉘"I'm afraid / you're mistaken, / Mr. Spencer," / said Ben Price. // ㉙"I don't believe / I recognize you." // ㉚Then / the big detective turned away / and walked slowly down the street. // (283 words) 🔊 意味のまとまりに注意して，本文全体を音読しよう！

New Words 新出単語の意味を調べよう

pain 名 [péɪn] B1	1.	despairing 形 [dɪspéərɪŋ]	2.

vest 名 [vést]	3.	drill 名 [dríl] A2	4.
bite 動 [báɪt] B1	5.	smoothly 副 [smúːðli] A2	6.
steel 名 [stíːl] B1	7.	completely 副 [kəmplíːtli] B1	8.
exhausted 形 [ɪgzɔ́ːstɪd] B1	9.	unharmed 形 [ʌnháːrmd]	10.
hesitate 動 [hézɪtèɪt] B1	11.		

A Comprehension
パラグラフの要点を整理しよう
Fill in the blanks in Japanese. 【思考力・判断力・表現力】

ジミー・バレンタインの行動と心境の変化

・(1.　　　　　　) がジミーに助けを求めた。

・ジミーは (2.　　　　　　) を脱いでスーツケースを開け，道具を取り出した。

・(3.　　　　　　) 分で金庫の扉を開け，アガサを助け出した。

・正体を知られたと思ったジミーは，その場を立ち去ろうと玄関に向かった。

・逮捕される覚悟をしたが，ベン・プライスは (4.　　　　　　) ふりをして去っていった。

B Key Sentences
重要文について理解しよう
Fill in the blanks and translate the following sentences.
【知識・技能】【思考力・判断力・表現力】

④ **"Can't you do something, Ralph? Try, won't you?"**

◆ 否定疑問文 Can't you 〜? は「〜できませんか。」の意味で，ここでは依頼や懇願を表す。

◆ 命令文の後に付加疑問 won't you? を加えて，強い期待の気持ちを表している。

訳 :

⑪ **With that act, Ralph D. Spencer disappeared, and Jimmy Valentine took his place.**

◆ that act とは，ジミーが (1.　　　　　　　　　　　　) ことを指す。

訳 :

⑲ **Agatha, / completely exhausted but unharmed, / ran into her mother's arms.**
S　　　　　　　　　　　　　　　　　　　　　　　　　　V

◆ 文中に挿入されている (completely) exhausted but unharmed は分詞構文で，アガサの状態を表している。形容詞 exhausted と unharmed の前には現在分詞 being が省略されている。

訳 :

Ask Friends and Followers for Advice on Social Media

教科書 p.156

🔊 意味のまとまりに注意して，本文全体を聞こう！

Nyanko //

①Our brass band practice is very hard / every day. // ②After practice, / I ride on the train / for about one hour / and get home late. // ③After I eat dinner / and take a bath, / it is already 9:30 p.m. // ④I'm always tired and sleepy! // ⑤How can I study? // ⑥Please give me some good advice. //

Yujin: ⑦Use your spare time wisely. // ⑧For example, / you can study / while you are on the train. //

Ribrib: ⑨Why don't you get up early / and study / in the early morning? // ⑩I do it. // ⑪It's really refreshing. //

David: ⑫You should tell your teacher / and other band members / about your problem. // ⑬They may give you good advice. // (108 words)

🔊 意味のまとまりに注意して，本文全体を音読しよう！

New Words 新出単語の意味を調べよう			
follower 名 [fá(:)louər] B2	1.	brass 名 [bræs] B1	2. (brass band)
spare 形 [spéər] B2	3.	wisely 副 [wáɪzli]	4.
Ribrib [ríbrɪb]	リブリブ	refreshing 形 [rɪfréʃɪŋ]	5.

Fill in the blanks in Japanese.

【思考力・判断力・表現力】

ニャンコの投稿		吹奏楽の練習が毎日大変。帰宅し，夕食を食べてお風呂に入ると午後9時半になっている。いつも疲れて眠い。どうやって(1.　　　　　　)したらいいかアドバイスがほしい。
コメント	ユウジン	空いた時間をうまく使って。(2.　　　　　　)の中で勉強できるよ。
	リブリブ	(3.　　　　　　)して勉強するととてもすがすがしいよ。
	デイヴィッド	(4.　　　　　　)やほかの部員に相談したほうがいい。

B **Key Sentences**
重要文について理解しよう

Fill in the blanks and translate the following sentences.

【知識・技能】【思考力・判断力・表現力】

③ **After I eat dinner and take a bath, it is already 9:30 p.m.**

◆ 接続詞andによって動詞eatとtakeが並列に結ばれている。

◆ 主節の主語のitは時間を表す用法で，「それ」とは訳さない。

訳：＿＿＿＿＿＿＿＿＿＿＿＿＿＿＿＿＿＿＿＿＿＿＿＿＿＿＿＿＿＿＿＿＿＿＿＿＿

⑧ **For example, you can study while you are on the train.**

◆ 接続詞whileは「…している間に」という意味の副詞節を導く。

訳：＿＿＿＿＿＿＿＿＿＿＿＿＿＿＿＿＿＿＿＿＿＿＿＿＿＿＿＿＿＿＿＿＿＿＿＿＿

⑨ **Why don't you get up early and study in the early morning?**
                              V₁   V₂

◆ Why don't you ～?は「～してはどうですか。」という提案や勧誘を表す表現。

◆ 2つの動詞getとstudyが接続詞andによって並列に結ばれている。

訳：＿＿＿＿＿＿＿＿＿＿＿＿＿＿＿＿＿＿＿＿＿＿＿＿＿＿＿＿＿＿＿＿＿＿＿＿＿

⑫ **You should tell your teacher and other band members about your problem.**

◆ 接続詞andによってyour teacherと 1.＿＿＿＿＿＿＿＿＿＿＿＿＿＿＿＿ が並列に結ばれている。

◆ tell＋人＋about ...は「人に…について話す」という意味。

訳：＿＿＿＿＿＿＿＿＿＿＿＿＿＿＿＿＿＿＿＿＿＿＿＿＿＿＿＿＿＿＿＿＿＿＿＿＿

Let's Buy Fair-trade Chocolate!

教科書 p.157

◀》 意味のまとまりに注意して，本文全体を聞こう！

You Can Make a Difference / in Farmers' Lives! //

① Chocolate may be your favorite food. // ② But do you know / growing cacao trees is hard work? // ③ Cacao trees grow / in hot, rainy, tropical places. // ④ Cacao plants are delicate. //

⑤ Small family farmers grow about 90% / of the world's cacao. // ⑥ They must protect trees / from wind, / sun, / insects / and illness. // ⑦ Cacao prices are rising, / but the farmers get very little / from its trade. // ⑧ The traders take away / much of the profit. //

⑨ Thanks to fair-trade, / cacao farming can be sustainable. // ⑩ We buy cacao beans / from those small farmers / at fair prices. // ⑪ We set up local funds, / too. // ⑫ Fair-trade has rules / about farming / to protect the environment. //

⑬ Why don't you buy fair-trade chocolate? // ⑭ That can be a great help / for cacao farmers. // (126 words)

◀》 意味のまとまりに注意して，本文全体を音読しよう！

New Words 新出単語の意味を調べよう			
leaflet 名 [líːflət] B2	1.	tropical 形 [trá(ː)pɪk(ə)l] B1	2.
delicate 形 [délɪkət] B1	3.	illness 名 [ílnəs] B1	4.
trade 名 [tréɪd] A2	5.	trader 名 [tréɪdər] B2	6.
profit 名 [prá(ː)fət] B2	7.	sustainable 形 [səstéɪnəb(ə)l]	8.
fund 名 [fʌ́nd] B1	9.		

Fill in the blanks in Japanese.

【思考力・判断力・表現力】

フェアトレードチョコレートの購入を呼びかけるリーフレット	
カカオ生産の現状	・カカオの木は熱帯地方で育ち，とても (1.　　　　　) なので育てるのが大変である。 ・90％のカカオの木が小規模な家族経営の農家によって育てられている。 ・カカオの価格は (2.　　　　　) しているが，貿易業者が (3.　　　　　) の多くを搾取しているため，農家の収入はとても少ない。
フェアトレードとは	・カカオ豆を小さな農家から (4.　　　　　) な値段で購入する。

⟶ フェアトレードチョコレートを買うことはカカオ農家の大きな助けになる。

B **Key Sentences**
重要文について理解しよう

Fill in the blanks and translate the following sentences.

【知識・技能】【思考力・判断力・表現力】

② **But do you know** <u>growing</u> **cacao trees is hard work?**
　　　　　　　　　　育てること

◆ growing cacao trees is hard work という節が動詞 1.＿＿＿＿＿＿ の目的語になっている。growing は動名詞。

訳：＿＿＿＿＿＿＿＿＿＿＿＿＿＿＿＿＿＿＿＿＿＿＿＿＿＿＿＿＿＿＿＿＿

⑦ **Cacao prices are rising, but the farmers get very little from its trade.**

◆ are rising は現在進行形で，「(価格が) 上昇している」ということ。

◆ its trade とはカカオ豆を売買する取引のこと。

訳：＿＿＿＿＿＿＿＿＿＿＿＿＿＿＿＿＿＿＿＿＿＿＿＿＿＿＿＿＿＿＿＿＿

⑫ **Fair-trade has rules about farming to protect the environment.**

◆ about farming は rules を後ろから修飾している。

◆ to protect は形容詞用法の不定詞で，rules (about farming) を修飾している。

訳：＿＿＿＿＿＿＿＿＿＿＿＿＿＿＿＿＿＿＿＿＿＿＿＿＿＿＿＿＿＿＿＿＿

⑭ **That can be a great help for cacao farmers.**

◆ That とは (2.　　　　　　　　　　　　　　　　　　) ことを指している。

◆ 助動詞 can は可能性を表す用法で，「～することもありうる」の意味。

訳：＿＿＿＿＿＿＿＿＿＿＿＿＿＿＿＿＿＿＿＿＿＿＿＿＿＿＿＿＿＿＿＿＿

Good to Be Different

教科書 p.158

🔊 意味のまとまりに注意して，本文全体を聞こう！

Reporter: ① What was the Rio Paralympics like / for you? //

Mei: ② I felt relieved / when I was chosen / for the Japanese team. // ③ People

hoped / I could get a medal, / but I knew / I wasn't good enough. //

Reporter: ④ After Rio, / you trained / in Australia / for three months. // ⑤ What

did you learn there? //

Mei: ⑥ Before that, / I just tried hard / to get a good result. // ⑦ On the other

hand, / Australian swimmers focused / on the quality / of their swimming. // ⑧ I

learned / to think logically / about my own performance, / and not just rely too

much / on feelings. //

Reporter: ⑨ Who had an impact / on your way / of thinking? //

Mei: ⑩ My mom and dad. // ⑪ They told me / it's good / to be different. // ⑫ I

hope / people see each person / as an individual. // (118 words)

🔊 意味のまとまりに注意して，本文全体を音読しよう！

New Words 新出単語の意味を調べよう				
competitive 形 [kəmpétətɪv] B1	1.		Rio [ríːou]	リオ（＝リオデジャネイロ）
logically 副 [lá(ː)dʒɪk(ə)li]	2.		rely 動 [rɪláɪ] B1	3.

A Comprehension

パラグラフの要点を整理しよう

Fill in the blanks in Japanese.

【思考力・判断力・表現力】

一ノ瀬メイ選手へのインタビュー	
Q.	リオパラリンピックはどうだったか。
A.	・日本代表チームに選ばれて(1.　　　　　)した。 ・メダルを期待されていたが，自分は(2.　　　　　)だとわかっていた。
Q.	リオパラリンピック後のオーストラリアでの練習で学んだことは何か。
A.	・オーストラリアの選手は泳ぎの(3.　　　　　)に目を向けていた。 ・泳ぎについて論理的に考えることと，感情に頼りすぎないことを学んだ。
Q.	一ノ瀬選手の考え方に影響を与えた人はだれか。
A.	・(4.　　　　　)。人と違っているというのはいいことだと教えられた。

B Key Sentences

重要文について理解しよう

Fill in the blanks and translate the following sentences.

【知識・技能】【思考力・判断力・表現力】

① **What was the Rio Paralympics like for you?**

◆ What is ... like?で「…はどのようなものか。」という意味。

訳：_____

② **I felt relieved** / when I was chosen for the Japanese team.
　S　V　　C

◆ 主節はS＋V＋Cの文。

◆ was chosenは受け身(過去形)であり，was chosen for ...で「…に選ばれた」という意味。

訳：_____

⑧ **I learned to think logically about my own performance, and not just rely too much on feelings.**

◆ learn to 〜で「〜できるようになる」という意味。

◆ and not just relyは，省略を補うとand learned not just 1._____ relyとなる。

訳：_____

⑪ **They told me it's good to be different.**

◆ They ＝ 2._____

◆ 形式主語itはto以下の内容を受けている。it is ... to 〜で「〜することは…である」の意味。

訳：_____

81

Welcome to an Esports Tournament!

教科書 p.159

🔊 意味のまとまりに注意して，本文全体を聞こう！

Dream Matches / Asian HS Tournament / by Sakura Gaming Online / — July 20 //

①Welcome to Dream Matches, / Asian HS Tournament / by Sakura Gaming. //

②This is a tournament / for Asian high school students / of all skill levels. // ③We are looking forward / to seeing the fighting spirit / of all players. // ④We thank you / for participating / in this exciting event! //

Date & Time: / Match 1 | July 20, 2021 | 6 p.m. //

Match 2 | July 20, 2021 | 7 p.m. //

Structure: / 25 Teams | 1 match //

Timezone: / Tokyo (UTC+9:00) //

Fees: / Free to play matches //

Rules: / ⑤1. Each team needs at least eight players / to participate. //

⑥2. All players / in the tournament / must have ESPORTS accounts. //

⑦3. Players must not use / any unofficial versions / of games. //

⑧4. Players must not use / unofficial items. //

⑨5. All team players must register / by the deadline. //

⑩After registration, / players will get more information / about the event. //

⑪Registration is now open / and will run / until July 20, / 2021, / 4 p.m. / JST. //

(155 words) 🔊 意味のまとまりに注意して，本文全体を音読しよう！

New Words 新出単語の意味を調べよう

participate 動 [pɑːrtísɪpèɪt] B1	1.	structure 名 [strʌ́ktʃər] A2	2.
timezone 名 [táɪmzòʊn]	3.	fee 名 [fíː] A2	4.
account 名 [əkáʊnt] A2	5.	unofficial 形 [ʌ̀nəfíʃ(ə)l] B2	6.
version 名 [vɚ́ːrʒ(ə)n] B2	7.	register 動 [rédʒɪstər] B1	8.
deadline 名 [dédlàɪn] B1	9.	registration 名 [rèdʒɪstréɪʃ(ə)n] B1	10.

A Comprehension パラグラフの要点を整理しよう　Fill in the blanks in Japanese.

eスポーツトーナメントの案内	
概要	あらゆるレベルのアジアの(1. 　　　　　　)を対象としたトーナメント
日時	2021年7月20日(第1試合：午後6時から，第2試合：午後7時から)
参加費	(2. 　　　　　　)
ルール	・各チーム(3. 　　　　　)名以上であること。 ・全選手がESPORTSアカウントを取得していること。 ・非公式バージョンのゲームや非公式(4. 　　　　　　)を使わないこと。 ・締め切り(2021年7月20日午後4時)までに登録をすること。

B Key Sentences 重要文について理解しよう　Fill in the blanks and translate the following sentences.

③ **We are looking forward to seeing the fighting spirit of all players.**

◆ look forward to 〜ingで「〜するのを楽しみにする」の意味。toに続くのは名詞または動名詞であることに注意。

訳：

⑤ **Each team needs at least eight players to participate.**

◆ each＋単数名詞で「各…，それぞれの…」の意味。

◆ participateの後にはin this tournamentが省略されている。

訳：

⑨ **All team players must register by the deadline.**

◆ mustは「〜しなければならない」という意味の助動詞。

◆ この前置詞byは「…までに」という期限を表す用法である。

訳：

⑪ **Registration is now open and will run until July 20, 2021, 4 p.m. JST.**
　　　　　S　　　V₁　　　C　　　　　V₂

◆ registrationは動詞 1.＿＿＿＿＿＿＿ の名詞形である。

◆ openはここでは「開いている，受け付けている」という意味の形容詞である。

◆ runはここでは「続く，継続する」の意味の動詞である。

訳：

"Favorite" Encounters

教科書 p.160

🔊 意味のまとまりに注意して，本文全体を聞こう！

①I was born / to an American father / and a Japanese mother. // ②I went to Yokohama International School. // ③Sometimes / it was challenging / for me / to communicate / in English / at school. // ④I first encountered the *koto* / at the age of nine. // ⑤I loved playing the musical instrument / during my first Japanese music classes / because I could make beautiful sounds / with it / easily. //

⑥I was first taught / by Mr. Patterson. // ⑦He has lived / in Japan / since 1986 / and performs / and teaches the *koto*. // ⑧He is a great teacher. //

⑨My classmates were impressed / with my playing / and this encouraged me / to work harder. // ⑩I realized / that it was easier / to express myself / through the *koto* / than with words. //

⑪I became a professional *koto* player / in 2017, / and now / I enjoy collaborating / with various artists. //　(130 words)　🔊 意味のまとまりに注意して，本文全体を音読しよう！

New Words　新出単語の意味を調べよう

encounter 名 動 [ɪnkáʊntər]　B1・B2	1. 名 動	Leo [líːou]	レオ
instrument 名 [ínstrəmənt]　A2	2.	challenging 形 [tʃǽlɪn(d)ʒɪŋ]　B1	3.
Patterson [pǽtərs(ə)n]	パターソン	express 動 [ɪksprés]　B1	4.
collaborate 動 [kəlǽbərèɪt]	5.		

箏曲家の今野玲央さんの投稿		
生い立ちと琴との出会い	・(1.) 人の父と日本人の母との間に生まれる。 ・インターナショナルスクールに通い，(2.) 歳のときに琴に出会う。 ・琴演奏家であるパターソン先生から琴を学ぶ。 ・(3.) よりも琴で自分を表現するほうが簡単だと気づいた。		
箏曲家としての活動	・2017年に (4.) の箏曲家になる。 ・さまざまなアーティストとの共同演奏を楽しんでいる。		

③ Sometimes it was challenging for me to communicate in English at school.

◆ it is ... to ～で「～することは…である」の意味。for meはto-不定詞の意味上の主語。

訳：_____

⑤ I loved playing the musical instrument during my first Japanese music classes / because I could make beautiful sounds with it easily.

◆ the musical instrumentとは具体的には (1. _____) のこと。itはthe musical instrumentを受けている。

◆ このwithは道具・手段を表し，「…を使って，…で」という意味。

訳：_____

_____

⑨ My classmates were impressed with my playing / and this encouraged me to work harder.

◆ thisは前半の節全体を指す。

◆ encourage＋人＋to ～で「人に～するよう励ます」という意味。

訳：_____

⑩ I realized that it was easier to express myself through the *koto* than with words.

◆ that-節中でto express myself through the *koto*と (to express myself) with wordsが比較されている。

訳：_____

Japanese Students Appeal for World Peace

教科書 p.161

🔊 意味のまとまりに注意して，本文全体を聞こう！

Japanese High School Students / Go to the U.N. //

① Do you think / young people have the power / to change the world? // ② Now, / the world knows / that some Japanese high school students / have worked hard / to help / to create a peaceful world. //

③ Japanese High School Student Peace Ambassadors / are chosen / every year / from around the country. // ④ They attend many conferences, / including one / at the United Nations Office. // ⑤ There, / they make speeches / in English / to appeal for world peace. // ⑥ They also submit signatures / they have collected / in support of the abolition / of nuclear weapons. //

⑦ In addition, / the ambassadors do some charity activities. // ⑧ They collect pencils and other stationery, / and they send them / to some poor countries. // ⑨ They also run a charity fund / for poor children / in Asia. //

⑩ In total, / more than 200 students / have worked hard / for peace / since 1998. // ⑪ Their voices have reached many people / around the world. //

(146 words) 🔊 意味のまとまりに注意して，本文全体を音読しよう！

New Words 新出単語の意味を調べよう

peaceful 形 [píːsf(ə)l] A2	1.	ambassador 名 [æmbǽsədər] B2	2.
attend 動 [əténd] B1	3.	conference 名 [ká(ː)nf(ə)r(ə)ns] B2	4.
United Nations [junàɪtɪdnéɪʃ(ə)nz]	国際連合	submit 動 [səbmít] B2	5.
signature 名 [sígnətʃər] B1	6.	abolition 名 [æbəlíʃ(ə)n] B1	7.
nuclear 形 [njúːkliər] B1	8.	weapon 名 [wép(ə)n]	9.
stationery 名 [stéɪʃənèri]	10.		

A **Comprehension**
パラグラフの要点を整理しよう

Fill in the blanks in Japanese.　　　　　　　　　【思考力・判断力・表現力】

世界平和のために尽力する日本人高校生	
高校生平和大使…日本中から毎年選ばれ，世界平和のために取り組んでいる。1998年以降，(1.　　　　　　)人以上の高校生が参加している。	
活動①	・国連事務局などでの会議に参加し，そこで平和を訴える英語の(2.　　　　　)を行う。 ・核兵器廃絶に賛同する(3.　　　　　)を集め，提出する。
活動②	・鉛筆などの(4.　　　　　)を集めて，貧しい国へ送る。 ・アジアの貧しい子供たちのための慈善基金を運営する。

B **Key Sentences**
重要文について理解しよう

Fill in the blanks and translate the following sentences.
【知識・技能】【思考力・判断力・表現力】

③ **Japanese High School Student Peace Ambassadors are chosen every year from around the country.**

◆ are chosen は受け身で，「選ばれ(てい)る」という意味。

◆ the country は具体的には日本のことを指している。

訳：

④ **They attend many conferences, including one at the United Nations Office.**

◆ including は「…を含めて」という意味の前置詞で，例示や補足を導いている。

◆ one は前出の名詞 1.＿＿＿＿＿＿＿ のくり返しを避けるために用いられている代名詞。

訳：

⑥ **They also submit signatures they have collected in support of the abolition of nuclear weapons.**

◆ they have collected は signatures を修飾している。signatures の後には目的格の関係代名詞 2.＿＿＿＿＿ が省略されている。in support of 以下の句も signatures を修飾している。

訳：

⑨ **They also run a charity fund for poor children in Asia.**
　　　 S　　　 V　　　 O

◆ S＋V＋O の文である。ここでの run は他動詞で，「…を運営する，…を管理する」という意味。

訳：

The Changing Meaning of "Convenience"

教科書 p.162

■)) 意味のまとまりに注意して，本文全体を聞こう！

①The number of convenience stores / in Japan / has been growing. //

②Convenience stores are easy / to drop into. // ③Their products are constantly

changing. // ④Every year, / about 70% / of all products / are replaced / by new

ones. // ⑤This is / because of demand / from society. //

⑥The customers of convenience stores / used to be mainly young people, / but

these days, / that is not the case. // ⑦According to the graph, / in 2017, / the

number of customers / aged 50 or over / was four times / as large as that / in

1989. //

⑧There will be more and more elderly people / in the future. // ⑨Home delivery

of products / will become more common / for people / who cannot travel easily. //

⑩They can order what they need online / and get it / at home. // ⑪As our

society is changing, / the meaning of "convenience" / can also change. //

(132 words)   ■)) 意味のまとまりに注意して，本文全体を音読しよう！

New Words 新出単語の意味を調べよう			
chart 名 [tʃáːrt] A2	1.	adapt 動 [ədǽpt] B1	2.
constantly 副 [ká(:)nst(ə)ntli] B1	3.	replace 動 [rɪpléɪs] A2	4.
delivery 名 [dɪlív(ə)ri] B1	5.		

日本でのコンビニ 増加の理由	・立ち寄りやすい。 ・社会の(1.　　　　　　　)を満たすため，商品が絶えず入れ替わる。
顧客層の変化	・かつては(2.　　　　　　)が中心だった。 ➡2017年には，50歳以上の顧客の数が1989年と比べて4倍に。
コンビニの あり方の変化	・高齢化に伴い，移動が困難な人のために商品の(3.　　　　　　　)が普及する だろう。 ・オンラインで注文し，(4.　　　　　　)で商品を受け取ることができる。

B Key Sentences
重要文について理解しよう

Fill in the blanks and translate the following sentences.
【知識・技能】【思考力・判断力・表現力】

② **Convenience stores are easy to drop into.**

◆ このto-不定詞は形容詞easyが示す範囲を限定している。この文は，It is easy to drop into 1.＿＿＿＿＿
＿＿＿＿＿＿＿＿＿＿＿＿＿＿＿＿＿ .と書きかえることができる。

訳：＿＿＿＿＿＿＿＿＿＿＿＿＿＿＿＿＿＿＿＿＿＿＿＿＿＿＿＿＿＿＿＿＿＿＿

⑥ **The customers of convenience stores used to be mainly young people, /**
but these days, / that is not the case.

◆ used to ～は「かつては～だった」という(現在と対比された)過去の状態を表す。

◆ thatは，コンビニの顧客が主に若者であるということを指している。

訳：＿＿＿＿＿＿＿＿＿＿＿＿＿＿＿＿＿＿＿＿＿＿＿＿＿＿＿＿＿＿＿＿＿＿＿
＿＿＿＿＿＿＿＿＿＿＿＿＿＿＿＿＿＿＿＿＿＿＿＿＿＿＿＿＿＿＿＿＿＿＿

⑦ **According to the graph, in 2017, the number of customers aged 50 or over**
was four times as large as that in 1989.

◆ four times as large as ...は，X times as ＋原級＋ as ...の形で「…のX倍～だ」という意味。

◆ aged 50 or overはcustomersを後ろから修飾している。

訳：＿＿＿＿＿＿＿＿＿＿＿＿＿＿＿＿＿＿＿＿＿＿＿＿＿＿＿＿＿＿＿＿＿＿＿
＿＿＿＿＿＿＿＿＿＿＿＿＿＿＿＿＿＿＿＿＿＿＿＿＿＿＿＿＿＿＿＿＿＿＿

⑩ **They can order what they need online and get it at home.**
　　S　　　V₁　　　　　　O　　　　　　　　　　　V₂　O

◆ what they needで「彼らが必要とするもの」という意味。whatは関係代名詞。

訳：＿＿＿＿＿＿＿＿＿＿＿＿＿＿＿＿＿＿＿＿＿＿＿＿＿＿＿＿＿＿＿＿＿＿＿

Machine Translation: No Need to Learn English?

教科書 p.163

🔊 意味のまとまりに注意して，本文全体を聞こう！

①Machine translation is simple. // ②The machine statistically finds out the most appropriate match / from translation data. // ③A set of data / is like: / "髪が長くなった; / My hair got longer." // ④It is broken up / into smaller pieces, / such as "髪; / my hair" / and "長くなった; / got longer." // ⑤When you put "日が長くなった" / into machine translation, / the machine matches the best pieces / of data / and produces "The day got longer." //

⑥However, / machine translation has several problems. // ⑦If translated sentences are inaccurate, / we must correct them. // ⑧In addition, / it is sometimes difficult / for us / to recognize inaccurate translations. //

⑨If we take an example, / like "部活で帰りが遅くなった," / we can see / how inaccurate sometimes machine translation is. //

部活で帰りが遅くなった。⇒ My return got late in club activities. //

⑩This machine translation is very unnatural. // ⑪You should say, / "I returned home late / because of my club activities." // ⑫So / it is still important / for us / to keep learning English hard. // (139 words)

🔊 意味のまとまりに注意して，本文全体を音読しよう！

New Words 新出単語の意味を調べよう			
translation 名 [trænsléɪʃ(ə)n] B2	1.	statistically 副 [stətístɪk(ə)li]	2.
appropriate 形 [əpróupriət] A2	3.	data 名 [déɪtə] B2	4.
translate 動 [trænsleɪt] B1	5.	inaccurate 形 [ɪnækjərət] B2	6.
unnatural 形 [ʌnnætʃ(ə)r(ə)l] B2	7.		

A **Comprehension**
パラグラフの要点を整理しよう

Fill in the blanks in Japanese.

【思考力・判断力・表現力】

機械翻訳のシステム：	
翻訳データから (1.　　　　　) 的に最も適切に一致する表現を見つける。	
問題点	・翻訳された文に誤りがあった場合，人間がそれを (2.　　　　　) しなければいけない。 ・不適切な翻訳を認識するのが (3.　　　　　) こともある。

　　　➡ 依然として英語の (4.　　　　　) を続けるのは大切である。

B **Key Sentences**
重要文について理解しよう

Fill in the blanks and translate the following sentences.

【知識・技能】【思考力・判断力・表現力】

④ **It is broken up into smaller pieces, such as "髪; my hair" and "長くなった; got longer."**

　◆ A is broken up into B は break up A into B 「AをBに分ける」が受け身になった形である。

　◆ such as A and B は「AやBのような，AやBなど」の意味で，具体例を導く表現である。

　訳：

⑦ **If translated sentences are inaccurate, we must correct them.**

　◆ if-節はS＋V＋C，主節はS＋V＋Oである。

　◆ translated は「翻訳された」という意味の過去分詞で，1.　　　　　　 を修飾している。

　訳：

⑨ **If we take an example, like "部活で帰りが遅くなった," we can see how inaccurate sometimes machine translation is.**
　　　　　　　　　　　　　　　　　　　　　　　　S　　V　　O

　◆ 主節はS＋V＋O (＝疑問詞節) である。

　訳：

⑫ **So it is still important for us to keep learning English hard.**

　◆ it is ... for A to ～「Aが～するのは…だ」の文である。形式主語 it は to 以下の内容を受けている。for us は不定詞の意味上の主語。

　◆ keep ～ing は「～し続ける」という意味。

　訳：

A Boy Helps to Solve the Microplastic Problem

教科書 p.164

🔊 意味のまとまりに注意して，本文全体を聞こう！

A Boy's Discovery / May Solve the Microplastic Problem //

①Microplastic pollution is a worldwide problem today. // ②A Canadian boy / has given us a good answer / to it. // ③Daniel Burd, / a 16-year-old high school student, / showed his research / on microbes / that could eat plastics. // ④He won the top prize / at the Canada-Wide Science Fair. //

⑤Daniel said, / "Plastics finally break down / and disappear, / though it usually takes 1,000 years / to do so. // ⑥This means / some microbes can eat plastics slowly." // ⑦Then / he asked himself, / "Can I make those microbes / do the job faster?" // ⑧He did his experiment / again and again. // ⑨At last, / he found the most powerful type / of microbe. //

⑩About 500 billion plastic bags / are used / worldwide / each year. // ⑪Billions of these end up / in the oceans. // ⑫Animals eat those plastic bags, / and as a result, / the animals often die. // ⑬Daniel's discovery will help us / solve the microplastic problem. // (147 words)　🔊 意味のまとまりに注意して，本文全体を音読しよう！

New Words 新出単語の意味を調べよう			
discovery 名 [dɪskʌ́v(ə)ri] B1	1.	worldwide 形 [wə̀:rl(d)wáɪd] B2	2.
Daniel Burd [dǽnjəl bə́:rd]	ダニエル・バード	Canada-Wide Science Fair [kǽnədəwàɪd sáɪəns féər]	カナダ全国科学フェア
experiment 名 [ɪkspérɪmənt] B1	3.	billion 形 名 [bíljən] B2	4. 形 名

A Comprehension
パラグラフの要点を整理しよう

Fill in the blanks in Japanese.

マイクロプラスチック問題の現状
・毎年世界中で約(1.　　　　　　)枚ものビニール袋が使われている。
・そのうちの何十億枚が海に流入している。

マイクロプラスチック問題解決につながる発見
・カナダの高校生がプラスチックを食べる(2.　　　　　　)に関する研究を発表した。
プラスチックが分解されるまでには通常(3.　　　　　)年かかる。
→微生物による分解を早くする方法を探して，何度も実験をくり返した。
→最も(4.　　　　　)なタイプの微生物を発見した。

B Key Sentences
重要文について理解しよう

Fill in the blanks and translate the following sentences.

【知識・技能】【思考力・判断力・表現力】

③ Daniel Burd, a 16-year-old high school student, showed his research on microbes that could eat plastics.

◆ Daniel Burdとa 16-year-old high school studentは同格関係である。

◆ thatは主格の関係代名詞で，that以下の節が先行詞microbesを修飾している。

訳：

⑤ Daniel said, "Plastics finally break down and disappear, though it usually takes 1,000 years to do so."

◆ thoughは「…だけれども，…にもかかわらず」という意味の接続詞。

◆ do so = 1.

訳：

⑦ Then he asked himself, "Can I make those microbes do the job faster?"
　　　　　　　　　　　　　　　S　V　　　　O　　　　C

◆ makeは使役動詞で，make＋O＋C（＝原形不定詞）で「OにCさせる」の意味になる。

訳：

⑬ Daniel's discovery will help us solve the microplastic problem.
　　　　S　　　　　　V　　O　C

◆ help＋O＋C（＝原形不定詞）で「OがCするのに役立つ」の意味になる。

訳：